TROUT
AND THE
SUBSURFACE
FLY

TROUT AND THE SUBSURFACE FLY

LOU STEVENS

SWAN·HILL
PRESS

First published in the UK in 1997
by Swan Hill Press, an imprint of Airlife Publishing Ltd

British Library Cataloguing-in Publication Data
A catalogue record for this book
is available from the British Library

ISBN 1 85310 872 3

Typeset by Phoenix Typesetting, Ilkley, West Yorkshire.
Printed in England by Livesey Ltd., Shrewsbury.

Swan Hill Press
An imprint of Airlife Publishing Ltd
101 Longden Road, Shrewsbury, SY3 9EB, England.

Foreword

The sport of flyfishing is blessed with an abundance of fine literature that can give hours of contemplative pleasure when we are not at the waterside. This literature can be divided into three main categories: anecdotal, historical and instructional. The anecdotal literature is often a joy to read, a perfect way to relax without overtaxing our mental processes. However, when we wish to improve our knowledge of the sport we invariably turn to historical or instructional literature.

The following pages are a mixture of all three types. It was not intended to be so when the writing commenced, but as the subject of the subsurface fly expanded it naturally evolved that way.

The fact that, as the research reported in the text shows, trout take 75–85 per cent of their food subsurface was reason enough for this work to be undertaken; in fact it made it absolutely necessary.

The historical background of the many types of subsurface flies, and the various methods of fishing them, naturally followed. And, as the necessity of describing fishing methods became apparent, I decided that I should describe actual past fishing situations and use anecdotes when they were useful. So we have a text that is a mixture – anecdotal, historical and instructional. Hopefully this format will present an enormously important subject in a readable form.

As a final point it must be stressed that it is not my intention to advocate the subsurface fly over other flyfishing methods – diverse situations demand diverse methods. However, since trout consume such a large percentage of their food subsurface, fishing the wet fly must take its very important place in the order of things.

So let us consider our subject in detail . . .

Lou Stevens
Alvaston
Derbyshire

For Katie, with my love.

Contents

List of Illustrations

Introduction

When we talk about trout and the subsurface fly, what we are really discussing is wet flyfishing in its many forms. Contrary to popular belief, fishing wet, if it is done properly, requires more skill than other forms of flyfishing. The fact that it can be performed badly and still take the odd fish is testimony to the effectiveness of the subsurface fly or lure.

The fly used may be one of many types: a traditional insect imitation, an attractor pattern, a fish-fry imitation, a lure or a nymph pattern. Lures may again be of several types, commonly called streamers, bucktails, matukas, zonkers, nobblers, etc. The total number of patterns one can choose from is almost beyond imagination.

Quite apart from the multitude of flies there are different species of trout. We have several varieties of rainbow, brook trout (actually a char), tiger trout (a hybrid) and leopard trout (another hybrid), none of which are indigenous to the UK; they are artificially bred in hatcheries for stocking purposes. In addition we have our own beloved indigenous brown trout and its sea-going cousin the sea trout. In fact, although it is said that rainbow trout do not breed naturally in the UK, there are two or three waters that do have a breeding population. However, generally speaking these fish are on the small side and do not attain the weight of hatchery-bred fish.

All these varieties of trout require a specific technique when presenting a wet fly, as they have widely different feeding habits. Their reaction to different types of wet fly must also be taken into account.

To add to the complexity, the type of water must also be

considered; you may be fishing a loch, a lough, a reservoir, a lake, a pond, a river, a stream, a brook etc. Each type of water not only requires a particular fly presentation technique, but the type and size of fly will necessarily vary from water to water.

So we have several variables:

* the fly
* the variety of trout
* the type of water

The permutations are almost endless.

The purpose of this book is to clarify your thinking, and I will attempt to do this by breaking down the problems into 'bite-sized' pieces. As has been said: 'Every problem is an opportunity in disguise.'

Chapter 1

The Quarry

A knowledge of our quarry, even a superficial one, is essential if we are to vary our tactics to suit the species we are pursuing, so here we will look at each type of trout individually.

Brown Trout

The common brown trout (*Salmo fario*), is often referred to as the wild brownie. This fish is a very ancient creature. Fossilised remains have been found that show it in the same form as today, so without doubt it has remained basically unchanged for many thousands of years.

Many anglers consider the brown trout to be an indigenous species to the UK, and in a sense they are right. It is indigenous, but it is not a species; it is only a subspecies. There is only one species that is indigenous to the UK, and that is the sea trout (*S. trutta*); *S.fario* is a non-migratory subspecies of this fish. At one time it was the fashion to classify as a separate species all those trout from different regions and locations in the UK that differed in coloration and shape. The list was endless. Then, many years ago, Dr Tate Regan, working out of the British Museum, investigated this muddle and brought some order to it. He found that the sea trout (*S. trutta*), was the only indigenous trout to the UK, and that all others were of the same species, regardless of differences in coloration, shape or location. True, these subspecies are often given a scientific classification, even today, but anglers must not be confused into thinking that they are fishing for anything other than varieties of *S.trutta*.

The colour of a brown trout can vary enormously – in fact it would be almost impossible to find two trout that were identical, even from the same water. The colour, which is due to a pigment, is influenced by the quality of the food available, the acidity or alkalinity of the water and the general health of the fish. Rich feeding results in large, brilliant spots. Where an abundance of very rich food is available the spots are so large that they tend to join together. Food that is rich in fats produces a substance called guanine, which makes the fish decidedly silver in appearance. Alkaline water (pH 7.6–8.4) is usually rich in underwater vegetation and insect life. The result is that the trout have a distinct silvery hue with large, brilliant spots. Acid water (pH 4–6.8) is usually poor in food supply and produces trout much darker in appearance with many small, well-defined spots. In peaty or muddy water the trout can be very darkly coloured.

There is a considerable difference, however, between a naturally dark fish from a water that normally produces dark fish, and the black appearance of a sick trout. Trout can suffer from many internal ailments, some brought about by parasites or just from old age. In all such cases they become either very pale, almost whitish in appearance, or so dark that they are almost black. Such trout are much better removed from the water if caught and should not be returned to contaminate healthy fish.

Brown trout begin to deteriorate at about seven years of age and from that point can be regarded as old fish. There have been reports of fish reaching over twelve years of age, but such instances are rare.

The size the fish attains in relation to its age depends entirely on its environment. As far as weight is concerned, a well-fed trout of 12 in (30 cm) will generally weigh about ¾ lb (340g), a 15 in (38 cm) trout 1½ lb (680 g) and one of 18 in (46 cm) will weigh 2½ lb (1.1kg).

Rainbow Trout

The rainbow trout, (a native of North America,) is found in many waters in the UK. In the main these are hatchery fish used as stock to be fished for on a 'put-and-take' basis. I know of only three rivers where it has become acclimatised and now thrives and spawns in the normal way. Apart from these, all rainbow stock-fish are hatchery bred by artificial means.

They are truly beautiful in appearance, predominantly silver with a myriad of black spots extending into the tail and a band of iridescent rainbow colours the length of the body – hence the name. In North America there are two species of these fish: *S.shasta* is the non-migratory species and *S.gairdneri* is the sea-going steelhead. In their natural habitat these fish grow to a considerable size, and weights in double figures are quite common. They were introduced into the UK in 1882, with no great care being taken as to which species were imported. The hatcheries in the UK also treated both species as identical; consequently, cross-breeding resulted during the artificial egg-stripping and fertilisation processes. The result is the cross-bred rainbow prevalent in the UK today, which is classified as *S. irideus*.

The rainbow trout is an aggressively greedy fish that consumes approximately twice the food of the brown trout, and puts on weight accordingly. A well-fed rainbow will increase in weight by well over 1 lb (450 g) per year, and hatchery-reared fish have exceeded that figure by a considerable margin. However, its life-span is short – very few rainbows live beyond six years of age. There is no doubt that it is an ideal stock-fish for 'put-and-take' stillwater fisheries.

When fishing for rainbows you should keep in mind the basic instincts that are peculiar to these fish. They are considerably more aggressive than browns and will often freely attack brightly coloured flies that the brown will not look at. They are also constantly on the lookout for food and are normally not nearly as selective as browns. When a hatch is in progress, however, they are as choosy as any other trout.

When rainbows are hooked they often become spectacular fighters – be prepared for a number of jumps out of the water. They are also very deceptive when they come to the net. Expect an apparently spent fish to come suddenly alive again, even jumping over the net!

Triploids

The triploid trout is essentially a rainbow that has been geneti-cally engineered in a hatchery. The result is that all triploids carry a double-X chromosome and are sterile females. The breeding procedure is a complicated one (way beyond my capability to explain fully), but a number of hatcheries are now able to carry out this procedure.

Most triploids are purchased for stock purposes by small private stillwater fisheries who are prepared to pay a little extra. Large waters, reservoirs etc. rarely bother.

There are distinct advantages for both fishery owners and anglers when triploids are stocked. Being sterile females they do not develop roe (eggs) during the breeding season; consequently they do not adopt breeding behaviour patterns. There is no fin and tail nipping and bullying, and no changes in physical condi-tion due to the breeding season. The result is that we have rainbows (albeit triploids) that are in first-class condition all year round. Small private stillwaters are able to offer flyfishing for twelve months of the year, and very often the winter months give outstanding sport. My own best rainbow, (12¼ lb 5.7 kg), was taken during a cold January only a week after Christmas. It was a triploid in terrific condition.

It has been noted during gutting that some triploids carry a trace of eggs, while others carry not only a trace of eggs but a sliver of milt at the same time. They are obviously sterile, but with a slight tendency towards bisexuality. Such abnormal-ities in no way affect their sporting quality – or their quality for the table.

Brook Trout

The brook trout (*Salvelinus fontinalis*) is not really a trout at all; scientifically speaking it is a char. This truly magnificent fish – its spawning colours are unbelievable – is a native of the eastern seaboard of the USA and Canada. It is the flyfisher's ideal: a fantastically beautiful appearance, a very strong fighter, a very free riser and a succulent meal on the table.

There is no reason why this fish should not establish itself in

Brook trout.   Two fine fish taken from a river in northern Canada.

the UK and breed naturally, but so far, results have been poor. It has been said that being a char, it needs very deep, cold water. This is not true, however. In its natural habitat the brook trout is often found in quite shallow rivers, many of which are quite warm during the summer months. I have caught wild brook trout in the Catskill mountains of New York State, in the Beaverkill River, during midsummer when the temperature was in the 70s. However, it is also true that the same region has an extremely cold winter, with an average temperature below zero.

A point worth noting is that the brook trout is fast disappearing from its natural habitat as civilisation encroaches. For really good wild brook trout fishing today one has to be prepared to fish wilderness areas. Obviously it requires a lot more than deep cold water.

Tiger and Leopard Trout

These fish are hybrids. Rainbows, browns and brook trout have been hatchery-crossed to the point that some spectacular hybrids have resulted. The natural colourings and markings of rainbows, browns and brook trout are ideally suited to obtaining these stunning results.

It cannot be stated with certainty that all these fish are, in fact, true trout. The use of brook trout (a char) in the process of crossbreeding makes it questionable that some of the resulting fish can really be classified as trout. However, such experimentation has only produced sterile fish, and there is therefore no question of a new strain becoming established. And from the standpoint of angling, there is no real difference. It is true that they may possibly have inherited some of the traits of their mixed parenthood, but such traits are difficult to determine.

These hybrids are mostly stocked by small private stillwater fisheries trying to give their customers something different and spectacular. Very few such fisheries will only stock the hybrids (it would be far too expensive), and the main fish stocked will probably be rainbows and perhaps a few browns. Fishing tactics should therefore be directed at the main stock-fish; the odd leopard or tiger trout will simply add spice to the day, particularly if you keep a camera handy!

Golden Trout

I have left this true trout until last not because it is rare – more and more small private stillwater fisheries are stocking them – but because it is nothing more than a specifically coloured rainbow.

Some golden trout are quite beautiful – strongly coloured golden orange with a very distinctive rainbow stripe. Others are somewhat anaemic, almost albino in appearance.

The most spectacular thing about golden trout is their appearance in the water. A true golden trout has no dark coloration along the back; it is golden all over, and consequently is very easily seen in the water, rather like goldfish in an ornamental pond. It gives an added dimension to the fishing, as they can be easily stalked and fished for individually.

However, when all is said and done these fish are true rainbows, and your tactics and fly choice should be determined accordingly.

Trout Food

Trout food consists mainly of living organisms that either live under water or are taken off the surface. By far the bulk of any trout's diet is taken underwater. The chief items of food taken are flies that are hatched from the water or fall to its surface, underwater larvae, small crustaceans, worms and leeches, small fish-fry and green algae. Most of these require clean and unpolluted water to thrive and flourish.

Colour is important. It must be remembered that the trout lives in a drab environment, and practically all its food is drably coloured. Although its colour vision cannot be doubted, it is not used to seeing bright, primary colours on a day-to-day basis; the primary colours of red, blue and yellow have no relationship to the colours that the trout normally associates with food. The secondary colours of green, olive and purple are more in keeping with its world, but by far the most natural to the fish are the tertiary colours of brown, olive and grey. When designing, tying or buying flies, this should be borne in mind.

Of course, flies tied in primary colours do have a place in our

19

fly box, especially for use as attractors. In some cases flies of these colours are used deliberately to induce a take.

The Trout's Senses

The senses of the trout cannot be related to our own, for the fish has a totally different bodily structure, designed for living in an underwater world. We can readily appreciate many of them; others are subject to conjecture.

The trout's lateral line and skin surface are made up of a complex nervous system that enables it to pick up vibrations over a considerable distance. The lateral line also enables it to ascertain the direction of the current and the pressure of the water. This latter facility helps it to avoid unseen obstacles when it is fighting to avoid capture.

Although vibrations are not the same as hearing as we know it, the result is practically the same. Aided by the earstones situated at the rear of its brain, the trout is able to 'hear' noises that cause even the slightest vibration. Footfalls on the bank, splashing water, dropped tackle, the impact of line on water – they are all 'heard' by the trout. External noises that cause no underwater vibration, however, such as talking, shouting or motor horns, are not picked up.

Trout have no sense of taste, as they have no taste buds. Their food is taken quickly by sight – taste does not enter into it at all. It would be completely useless to try to give an artificial fly any sort of flavour. However, trout do possess olfactory organs that pick up odours. They are attracted by some odours and repelled by others. This sense is entirely different from that of an air-breathing animal and has no connection with the breathing process itself, which, in the case of the trout, is performed through the gills.

It is often said that the trout's sense of vision is acute. However, it has no means of adjusting the pupils of its eyes as a protection against bright light, nor has it eyelids or eyelashes to shade the eyes. Consequently, bright light has a dazzling effect. It has no binocular vision to help it judge distances, and the panoramic vision it does possess makes it impossible to focus both eyes at the same time on a particular object. The eyes are also tilted forwards and upward so that it is practically impossible to see objects below and behind it.

Nevertheless, be in no doubt that its eyesight is perfectly designed for its needs; it is up to us to take advantage of the deficiencies. When fishing, try to keep the sun behind you, making sure, of course, not to cast a shadow over the fish. At the same time remember that a fly cast to a shaded area is seen much more acutely than one that is seen in bright sunlight, which slightly dazzles the trout. As our business is to deceive, the less chance we give the trout for close examination the better.

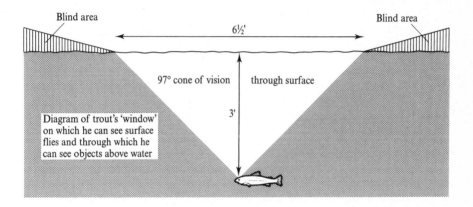

FIGURE 1   The trout's window (1)

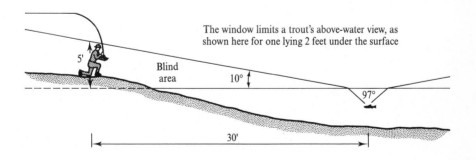

FIGURE 2   The trout's window (2)

21

Owing to the trout's cone of vision (see Figures 1 and 2), an angler some 30 ft (9 m) from the fish is invisible, provided no part of him is more than 5 ft (1.5 m) above water level. Since an angler's upper torso when wading is considerably less than that height above water level, we can approach the trout in the assurance that we cannot be seen within a 10 yard (9 m) cast. However, be warned: although we cannot be seen, the vibrations we make are a different matter and can be picked up by the fish long before we are within casting distance.

Chapter 2

The Reactions of Trout

Before we consider the different reactions of different varieties of trout, we must be very clear why these reactions take place.

Trout usually take wet flies for one of four reasons. First, they may assume it is edible and they are hungry. Secondly, they may not be hungry but still take the fly out of curiosity, because it does not represent a known natural food form but behaves in a similar manner. Thirdly, a trout is not a docile creature – in fact it is quite aggressive. Very often a fly is struck, and struck hard, out of pure aggressive anger at its intrusion into the trout's personal space. This is particularly true of some of the more gaudy lures when rainbows are the quarry. Brook trout and the hybrids are even more aggressive than rainbows.

We very often overlook the fourth reason, which is a playful, almost spiteful attitude towards a smaller creature. We often see such behaviour by a cat towards a mouse or bird, especially if the small creature seems to be injured. The cat may be very well fed, but it will still play with its miserable prey. A trout is no different; even a well-fed trout will sometimes strike at a fly that appears, by its swimming action, to be in distress. Most anglers have seen trout slashing at flies they have no intention of devouring. Sometimes they even return to it for a second attack.

These different reasons, whilst they present the fisherman with a quandary, offer a splendid opportunity to adopt a selective attitude towards fly patterns. If a good imitative pattern is ignored it is an indication that either the trout is not hungry or the imitation has not deceived it. If the fly is still ignored after a change of imitative pattern then the situation could well call for a change of tactics.

We do not have to know the fish's specific mood. If it is not hungry, then we need a fly pattern that will bring an angry, a curious or a playful response – in other words an attractor pattern that is very different from an insect or fish-fry imitation. It makes little difference to the angler what causes the fish to strike as long as a strike can be induced. But although this applies to all varieties of trout, not all varieties respond to a given situation in the same manner.

The Different Reactions of Different Varieties

Brook trout and hybrids, the tiger and leopard trout, are notoriously naive. A brightly coloured and tinselled fly is very attractive to them. Obviously, their curiosity, temper and spitefulness are highly developed.

By contrast, the brown trout is far less inclined to be curious. It does show considerable aggression when its space is violated, but, generally speaking, a good insect imitation is usually more effective for brown trout. The so-called ferox brown trout is an exception. A very large fish and a confirmed cannibal, the ferox is usually found at great depths in quite large stillwaters. Only a metal spinning spoon or a fly that is a large lure (a bait-fish imitation) has much chance of success.

But very few large browns are ferox. A number of large stillwaters hold browns weighing many pounds. Some reservoirs are stocked with both browns and rainbows in double-figure weights. Generally such large browns are confirmed insect eaters and will happily take a small fly that is a good insect imitation. I once took a 6¼ lb (2.8 kg) brown on a size 14 black gnat.

Rainbow trout, being such heavy feeders, spend nearly all their time searching for food. Whilst good imitations are, of course, very acceptable, anything that looks like an edible bug and moves is often investigated and sampled. The rainbow seems to feed on the principle that everything ought to be tried then rejected if not edible. In addition rainbows are very curious and will certainly attack items that suddenly attract their attention.

24

Quite large, gaudy flies are often very successful for rainbows.

Many anglers believe that a large lure intended to imitate a bait-fish is ideal for large rainbows. It is thought that rainbows are avid fish-fry eaters. Perhaps this belief stems from reported sightings of rainbows chasing schools of fish-fry, aptly called 'fry bashing'. At one time I was also of this opinion, having a number of times seen large fish attacking shoals of fry at the local reservoir. So ferocious were these attacks that many dead fry were left floating on the surface. It was quite a surprise to discover that the predators were, in fact, large perch hunting as a pack.

Nevertheless, large rainbows certainly do eat small fry. There are many instances of fry being found in their stomachs during gutting. However, it does not happen as often as we tend to believe. Most of our large lures are not taken as food items, but are attacked out of aggression and curiosity.

There is another point that needs to be made. When hatchery-bred browns and rainbows are used as stock fish in the same water – a common occurrence when reservoirs are stocked – the fish seem to develop similar reactions to wet flies. It is likely that their earlier life in hatchery surroundings has more influence than we think, and that, regardless of the passage of time since stocking, the fish are never truly wild.

Without doubt a stocked rainbow is easier to catch than a wild brown. Sometimes the newly stocked rainbow is so easy to take on almost any fly that very little skill is required. Whilst this is an ideal situation for the induction of a beginner to flyfishing, the experienced angler should look for a greater challenge. All flyfishers need to progress beyond yanking out newly stocked rainbows from a small pond.

But even small stocked ponds have fish in them that have survived for some time since stocking, that may even have wintered over. They will have put on weight and prove worthwhile adversaries, and they are worth pursuing. Their mood reaction can be worked out, and the fly patterns can be selected accordingly and fished with the action necessary to induce a take. So leave the newly stocked fish to swim around in circles and be caught by the novices who need the encouragement.

Regardless of the type of wet fly selected never forget that it should be fished in accordance with your assessment of the mood of the fish. For example, if fish are on the feed and you are presenting an imitation of a natural insect, then fish it in the manner a natural insect would behave. Natural insects do not move through water at 10 mph! A few inches per minute would be more in keeping. On the other hand if you are fishing a flashy attractor pattern, hoping to induce an aggressive strike, a rapid, irregular retrieve would be in order. Think the situation through, decide the mood of the fish, select the appropriate pattern, then fish it in a manner to achieve your objective.

Weather

Weather also dictates strategy. Very cold days are not inducive to fishing fast-moving flies; the fish are sluggish and their movements slow. At the same time they may be hungry and a larger fly might tempt them to move if it is fished slowly.

In very hot weather trout suffer from a lack of oxygen in the water which makes them almost dormant. I remember one such day on a Canadian lake when the temperature was in the high 80s, and had been for several days. All the trout, hundreds of them, had gathered at the mouth of a smaller feeder stream and were lying in only a few inches of water, which was apparently better oxygenated. It was like a huge carpet of trout, and nothing would make them move; it would have made little difference if I had waded among them – hopeless fishing conditions.

However, a warm sunny day is altogether a different proposition. Fish cruise all day, keeping an eye open for food. The problem is one of presentation. The fish will probably be high in the water; they will see you very well and bad casts will be visible a mile away. Moreover all flies are clearly seen in the good light. This is the time to think of small natural imitations fished very slowly just below the surface – the slower the movement the greater the chance of success. In fact, sometimes, even stationary flies will be picked off just below the surface.

So the moods of the fish cause different reactions, and we need to assess the mood to select the right fly or lure. Then we need to fish the selected fly or lure in the correct manner, in accordance with the reaction expected. And we should always bear in mind the effect of weather on our presentation.

Chapter 3

Traditional Wet Flies

Since ancient times fish have been caught on lures made of feathers. In the UK, during the Middle Ages, the use of artificials to catch trout was not unknown. Drawings of trout flies in the fifteenth century show flies remarkably similar to those used today.

To these earlier patterns so many others have been added that the choice today is vast. It is almost impossible to think of a colour combination, or a combination of materials, that has not already been used.

A study of these numerous patterns makes one realise that very little has been done to imitate natural insect life – nearly all patterns are designed purely to attract. The theory seems to be that if one combination of colours will not attract, another will. Quite a number of these flies have been named after particular insects, but this is mostly due to the colours used and has very little to do with any attempt at imitation.

Why Trout Take Flies

This leads one to ask, why trout take these flies. We do not know, and that is the root of the problem. If we knew the answer we would be able to evolve new and better wet flies, instead of which the so-called 'new' wet flies one sees are nothing more than the old combinations rehashed into different permutations. We are forced to conclude that if these flies take fish, then something about them must deceive the fish. We can be certain of one thing – they are not taken because they so closely resemble the natural insect that the fish cannot tell the difference!

The Woolly Worm.   A very old pattern.

It would be easy to suggest that the flies create an *illusion* of the natural insect, which is itself not very clear, and that the illusion is a very good imitation of what the trout normally expects to see. However, this is just not so; the wet fly is under water, in the trout's own medium, and is very clearly visible. It is amazing how often, in this type of discussion, one comes full circle without finding an answer. Why do the trout take these artificials? If only we knew!

29

One theory that seems sound is that the reason a trout takes a wet fly may differ each time it is taken, depending entirely on what movement the fly was making at that time. Obviously the fly is taken as something edible and, depending on its behaviour at the moment it is taken, imitates the type of food it is believed to be by the trout. A wet fly on a free drift downstream could, perhaps, be taken as a drowned terrestrial insect, as a drowned aquatic fly, as a free-swimming nymph, or as a slow-moving small fish-fry. A wet fly that is being manipulated to dart about could be confused with a darting nymph, or more likely with a small fish-fry. When the wet fly is rising to the surface in a sweeping arc, it is probably taken as a nymph rising to hatch, but it could also be taken as a fast moving fish-fry. There are also many other subaquatic creatures that have to rise to the surface periodically to breathe air.

So perhaps the colours and the tinsel ribbing of these flies do serve a purpose, even if we are not fully aware of what that purpose is. Under the various conditions in which they are seen by the trout, together with their varied motions through the water, perhaps at a particular moment they truly represent what the trout imagines them to be.

Many of the flies used today in the UK originated in the USA, for hundreds of patterns have now crossed the Atlantic. Most flies from the USA were designed to take native US trout (rainbows, brook trout etc.) that are notoriously naive compared with our native browns. Reservoir flyfishers have found many of the US patterns first class for the stocked rainbows.

A vexed question is how many wet flies to use on a leader. Many years ago it was standard procedure to use multiple flies tied on droppers standing out from the leader. In fact, this is still very much accepted practice on Scottish and Irish stillwaters, and many reservoir anglers adopt the same procedure with quite good results. On a small stream, however, the disadvantages are so great that the multiple system is not worthwhile. We have enough bankside and overhead vegetation to overcome – to say nothing of underwater snags – without giving ourselves further items to snag up. It is a matter of individual choice.

Choosing Wet Flies

When it comes to choosing a selection of wet flies for the fly box, only general advice can be offered. Many patterns have over the years become household names and are proven takers of fish. This applies mostly to the older patterns that were specifically designed for river use, or to the traditional loch patterns. Although the loch patterns will often take fish in a stream, they are most useful in high and coloured water, and when they are tied on much smaller hooks than is the usual loch practice.

There are so many wet flies to choose from, representing a multiplicity of food forms, but good initial selection would include traditional patterns as first choice, with stillwater patterns for river use if they are sparsely dressed and on hooks smaller than size 12.

The various regions of the UK have local patterns that have evolved over the years. They are not necessarily new patterns but old ones tied in a particular way (see Figures 3 and 4). Regional flies should always be considered in the region concerned, as they have evolved for very good reasons.

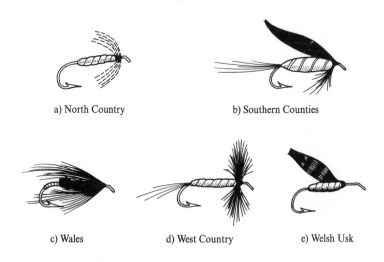

a) North Country   b) Southern Counties

c) Wales   d) West Country   e) Welsh Usk

FIGURE 3 Regional wet flies

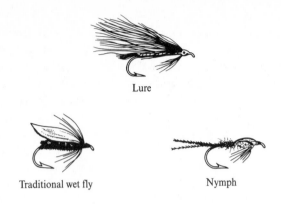

FIGURE 4   Types of wet fly

Weighting

Finally, we should discuss the weighting of flies. It is often necessary to fish a fly considerably deeper than it would normally
work. Sinking lines help in this situation, but a leader several
yards long somewhat negates the advantage.

The practice of pinching a small lead shot on the leader ahead
of the fly is far from satisfactory. First, even the smallest shot is
usually far too heavy and prevents the fly working properly.
Secondly, casting is adversely affected, particularly roll casting.
Furthermore it is difficult to make a cast with finesse.

The weighted fly is a far better proposition, provided the
weighting is kept to a minimum. It is surprising how little
weight is required – often a layer of fine copper wire on the
hook shank prior to tying the fly is quite sufficient. The addition
of a wire rib would add additional weight. Some flytiers use
lead wire on the hook shank, but this is rather drastic in the
case of small traditional flies, and results in a fly that is far too
bulky to make a smooth entry through the surface film of the
water.

A modern approach to the weighting problem is the use of soft
impregnated polymer (sold under a variety of trade names) on
the leader. The advantage over lead shot is that the smallest

amount can be used, just a smear along a couple of inches of the leader, and casting is hardly affected.

Before we leave the subject of weighted flies we must stress that the tippet used must be upgraded (i.e. it must have a thicker diameter), otherwise good fly presentation will be impossible. Moreover, a weighted fly is capable of snapping a fine tippet during the casting process.

Chapter 4

Fishing Traditional Flies in Deep Water

By far the best way to explain any technique is to give a practical demonstration at the same time. So I am going to invite you to come fishing. The situations we shall encounter are not imaginary, and I hope to pass on the experience that was gained at the time.

Deep Stillwater

Today we will fish at a small private stillwater fishery that is stocked with rainbows. The lake covers approximately 2 acres and is shaped roughly like a frying pan (see Figure 5). After several days of heavy rain the weather has now improved, and the water is on the high side and just a little coloured. As we look over the lake there is no obvious fish movement. We have already fished the shallow area A to B without result, so the decision is made to move to area C, where the water is much deeper.

Area C is actually the outlet for the lake and a small concrete dam has been built. The water at the dam face is about 12 ft (30.5 m) deep. We will fish off the bank to the side of the dam where the water is a little shallower.

We could use a fast-sinking line and fish our flies close to the bottom; a lot of anglers would do just that, and fish a large, gaudy lure with a fast line stripping retrieve. However, we consider it more prudent to work on the situation slowly until we can assess the depth at which the fish can be located. We start with a slow-sinking line and a large Hare's Ear nymph that has gold tinsel ribbing added for flash and visibility. We will 'fan-cast' the area

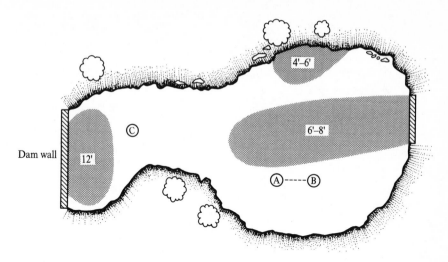

FIGURE 5   A small private stillwater

(see Figure 6), and use a slow hand-twist retrieve. Each cast will be 'counted down' to a different level.

This counting down procedure is not difficult to master. The cast is made, then a slow count started as the line sinks. At the end of each count, a slow retrieve commences. Different manufacturers' lines sink at different rates but most slow-sinking lines sink at an approximate rate of 2½ in (6 cm) per second. Most regular fast-sinking lines sink at an approximate rate of 5 in (13 cm) per second. So if we count at approximately one-second intervals then on the count of five a slow-sinking line will be at a depth of approximately 12 in (30 cm), and a fast-sinking line at 24 in (60 cm).

We are, of course, hoping for a take, but a slight pull will also serve our purpose. We need to know at what depth the fish are moving; once that is established we can continue to fish on the same count, changing flies if necessary.

It must be appreciated that most types of sinking line do not sink at a uniform rate throughout their length. The heavier middle section, or belly, will sink at the approximate rate given above, but the lighter tip section will be higher in the water. The addition of a light leader will not improve the situation as

35

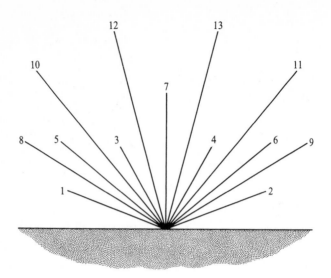

FIGURE 6   Fan-casting stillwater. Note the order in which the casts are made.

the light leader will sink at an even slower rate than the tip section of the line. So if we want to have the fly working at the depth the count indicates, then the fly itself must be weighted. At least with a weighted fly we are able to maintain the belly of the line, the tip section and the leader at roughly the same depth.

We have been lucky. After the fourth cast (count of thirty), we get a gentle pull, but miss the fish. We now know several things. The fish are about a third of the depth off the bottom, they are interested in food (our fly was not attacked, just gently mouthed and rejected), and our rate of retrieve is about right. Let us therefore try a smaller version of the same fly, fished on a count of thirty with a slightly slower retrieve.

Half an hour later we have three nice fish on the bank, but there have been no offers to the last dozen casts. It is time to move location.

Did you notice the chap fishing off the dam? His line was well down, probably a fast sinker, and he was retrieving in long, fast pulls. He has not had a single fish, yet he is still there using the same tactics.

36

Deep Running Water

Today we will fish the river. The sun is shining, not a cloud in the sky, the temperature in the low 70s. The water is very clear and low, very inviting. It is a lovely day – or is it? From our point of view it could be a lot better. It is far too bright and the water is too low and clear. We can see the stream-bed quite clearly, and even using our polaroids no fish are visible. Except for a few black gnats over the water there are no signs of insect life. There will probably be a good hatch of pale wateries later on, perhaps when the sun has gone down, but for now nothing is showing, not even a few spinners from an earlier hatch. The best thing we can do is to walk along the bank and look for some deep water.

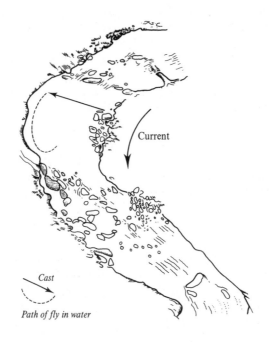

FIGURE 7   Fishing a deep-water bend

This curve in the river (see Figure 7) looks promising. The opposite bank is a high limestone escarpment and the water at its base looks very deep indeed. It has a cold green look and we can see where the stream-bed slopes away into the depths. It is impossible to say how deep it is, but the river generally is between 1½ and 3 ft (0.5–1 m), with the stream-bed clearly visible. Although the deep water is obviously different, I doubt whether it is more than 6–8 ft (1.8–2.4 m). The current and odd flooding would slowly fill a hole that was any deeper.

On a day like this it is not difficult to imagine a few nice browns lying deep and cool in that hole, away from the glaring sun. They are probably not on the feed, but keeping a wary eye open for the odd titbit brought directly to them by the current.

We will not need a sinking line; in fact it would be a hindrance. Our floating line with a 12 ft (3.6 m) leader will suit our tactics very well. We will need a heavy fly to get down to any fish, so we will start operations with a leaded Woolly Worm, although any 'buggy' leaded fly would probably be just as good. A sparsely dressed fly or nymph will not serve, as we require weight. We must also remember to change our tippet to 2x or 3x, as a light tippet is out of the question with a weighted fly.

Now for our tactics. If we cast upstream of the deep bend, as far upstream as we can, our weighted Woolly Worm will have time to get well down by the time it reaches the deep water opposite. With luck it will be rolling along on the bottom and pulling the tip of the floating line down below the surface.

Our problem will be knowing if the fly is taken. We are bound to have some slack in the line – with this type of tactic it cannot be helped – so we will not be able to feel any take. Watching the tip of the line might help, but it will only just be visible below the surface. But, we can overcome the problem with some brightly coloured wool I have in my bag. A short doubled-over length can be tied in a bow at the leader/line connection; it will be pulled under the surface but remain highly visible, and, it will not affect the casting in any way.

Within seconds of our cast landing the line is swept downstream into the deep bend, and, after a moment's delay, away downstream. Everything happens so quickly! Next time we will be ready and control the line with a mend upstream; in that way we will get the fly to linger a little longer in the deep water.

Now we can see what is happening. Although the tip of the line is well below the surface and only just visible, the bright yellow wool can be clearly seen. On our fourth drift through the bend the wool jerks downwards, out of sight. It could be a snag, but we tighten anyway. A hard strike is needed as we have slack line to overcome.

And that is the way to take a lazy brown out of a deep hole on a warm sunny day!

Chapter 5

Fishing Traditional Flies in Shallow Water

Shallow Stillwater

Once again we will visit our small private stillwater (see Figure 5 on page 35) but this time we will fish the shallow area A to B.

But although the area is shallow, it is not the same depth throughout. Figure 5 shows the different depths that confront us. The generally shallow areas, approximately 3 ft (1 m) deep, will require a different technique from the deeper areas, which are between 4 and 8 ft (1.2–2.4 m) deep.

Because of the shallowness of the area we need to be very aware of the effect of our presence on the trout. They will see us some time before we see them. It would therefore be best if we tackled up a few yards back from the bank, and made sure we avoided causing any vibrations.

In fact, we will commence our fishing operations about 8 yd (7 m) back from the bank, but more about that later.

The first thing is to decide which line to use. The shallows are better fished with a line that will enable us to control the depth of fly within very close limits, and at the same time will not leave a wake on the water surface to scare the fish. This rather rules out both fast-sinking and floating lines, so we are left with the possibility of using a slow sinker, a sink-tip or an intermediate line.

Sink-tip lines are enigmas. They do not cast very well because of the change in density along their length. They also act either as a sinking line with a buoyancy handicap or as a floating line with a sinking handicap. An intermediate line would be first class for fishing in the surface film or just below the surface, and would not leave a wake as we retrieve. However, it would be almost impossible to control the depth of the fly in the deeper areas. No. The tactics we will have to adopt for varying depths up to 8 ft (2.4 m), are much better served with a slow-sinking line.

Next we must decide on a suitable fly. Again the depth of water must be taken into consideration; the fish will be able to see very clearly whatever fly we use, and although rainbows are our quarry a large fancy lure would really look out of place and could possibly even scare the fish. Moreover, large flies cause some disturbance when they land on the water surface, which is not at all desirable in such shallow water. After some thought we decide on a small fly, a size 14 Coachman will be a good start.

We are now ready to commence operations and will fan-cast each area in turn (see Figure 6 on page 36), but first we must pay attention to the shallow margins close to the bank. Many good fish browse close to the bank in very shallow water when there is no-one on the bank to disturb them, but as soon as anyone approaches they scoot off to deeper water and safety.

We will make our first few casts from our present position, some 8 yd (7 m) back from the bank. We will cast over the grass so that only the fly and leader land on the water surface. In this way we can explore the margins thoroughly before moving closer to the water's edge.

Our tactics pay off; after a few casts we have a nice rainbow that took our fly quite close to the bank. That fish would not have been there if we had walked straight up to the bank to commence our operations.

We continue by fan-casting from the bank, exploring all other areas using the count down principle. Our retrieve must be very slow, less than a couple of inches per second, as natural insects move much more slowly than we believe.

Before long we encounter an aggravating problem. At times the fly is not sinking, especially after a couple of false casts, and giving a sharp pull to make it sink is disturbing the water. The best thing to do is to look around for some mud – if the banks are dry scoop up water with your hand and mix it with some dry soil. When you have made up a quantity of very wet mud rub the fly

41

hard into it, then rinse it off at the water's edge. It will be some time before a fly treated in this manner begins to float again, and very often a fly that has been roughed up a little is more attractive to the fish.

The combination of line selection, fan-casting, count down, fly selection plus a very slow retrieve have resulted in a number of fine fish being taken under quite difficult conditions.

Shallow Running Water

Shallow running water, or thin water as it is called by our American cousins, is usually one of two types. It can be turbulent over a rocky or stony stream-bed, commonly called riffles, or smooth, slick water, often referred to as flats. Good fish can be found in both types of water, but the fishing techniques required are very different if they are to be taken.

Turbulent shallow water has an uneven stream-bed; that is the reason for the surface turbulence. Consequently there are many sheltered lies for the fish. It is surprising how a small rock or a large stone will give shelter out of the current to a good-sized fish. Fish mostly lie behind such rocks, hugging the stream-bed, but sometimes a position is taken in front of a rock. The front position not only offers relief from the current but is also a good feeding station (see Figures 8 and 9).

Flats may be smooth water or have a good slick current. Because of the exposure to danger, fish are very wary in such areas during feeding sessions. Fish will very often move into the flats looking for food just after dawn or at dusk. Once the light has gone they will cruise the flats in a much more confident manner.

We will make a start by fishing the riffles. It will be best to use a floating line with a leader not exceeding 9 ft (2.7 m). A sinking line, or a longer leader, could snag on the submerged rocks and cause difficulties. Whether or not more than one fly is used is a matter of personal choice. Multiple flies on droppers are likely to snag more often than a single fly, but they do increase the chance of a fish. If stouter nylon is used for the dropper and the droppers are kept short (say about 3 in (75 cm), snagging can be kept to the minimum.

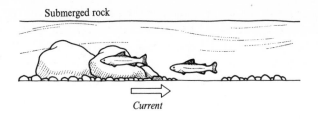

Submerged rock

Current

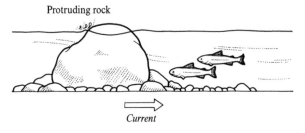

Protruding rock

Current

FIGURE 8   The natural feeding lies of trout

The turbulence on the surface caused
by the rock appears a little downstream
of the rock's true position

Current

FIGURE 9   Turbulence in a riffle shows the
position of underwater fish lies

The section of river we are going to fish has a strong current
and considerable surface turbulence, and the depth is a fairly
constant 2–3 ft (600cm–1 m). Clearly the stream-bed is quite
rocky. Careful wading would be possible, but it is not necessary
as the river is not very wide. We will use a 9 ft (2.7 m) leader with
one fly on the point and one dropper 3 ft (1 m) above. This rig

43

might give the impression of a small fish chasing a natural fly. A good point fly might be a mini-lure (a size 14 Thunder Creek type, see Chapter 11), with a traditional wet fly on the dropper. A personal choice for the dropper might be one of the spider-type wet flies, perhaps a Partridge and Orange spider.

FIGURE 10   Quartering a cast downstream

We can fish by quartering the flies downstream or by using a standard upstream cast. By moving downstream a few paces after every three casts we will cover the complete length of the riffle (see Figures 10 & 12).

Our flies will be carried by the current in a free drift. If you wish you can feed a little extra line through the rod rings so that the distance of the free drift is extended. As the flies reach the limit of the drift, the current will swing them to the centre of the stream. Because of the length of free drift, the flies will have sunk quite deeply in the water. At the end of the drift, the flies will

44

head towards the surface in a rising arc. We hope the impression will be that of a nymph or fly heading for the surface and being chased by a small fish.

Once the flies are at the centre of the stream, we can pause and let them play in the current, perhaps drawing in a little line then letting it out again so that the flies swim against the current then fall back.

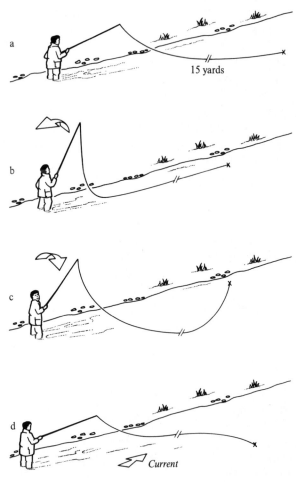

FIGURE 11   Sweeping a pool

We can now try a short retrieve in a series of sharp pulls. The retrieve can be followed by the draw and release that we first used, followed by another short retrieve. We are in no hurry to cast again. Flies in the water are working, so we will leave them there as long as possible, giving them movement by constant manipulation.

When we are ready to cast again we will move a few paces downstream so as to cover new water. With luck we will take one or two fish before we reach the end of the riffle.

There is another way of fishing wet flies down a long riffle that originated in the USA. It resulted from watching small boys fishing the Beaverkill River in the Catskill Mountains of upper New York State, and is called sweeping. The description might sound somewhat complicated, but if you refer to Figure 11 as you read the text it should become quite clear.

We let the line out downstream so that about 15 yd (13.5 m) is extended in the current, as in position (a). We are then ready to start. The line is drawn in by raising the rod tip until a loop of line is hanging down, as in position (b). The rod is then swung over to the right so that a well-curved line is on the water, as in position (c). Without any effort on our part this curve will straighten out in the current and swing the fly to the right. As the fly swings to the right it will rise to the surface in an arc. When the fly has completed its swing to the right it will then swing back towards the left until we are once again in position (a).

The line is again drawn in (position (b)), and the procedure repeated, swinging the rod tip to the left, as in position (d). This time the fly swings to the left in a rising arc again.

Once we have swept fully to the left and to the right, it is time to wade forward a couple of paces and repeat the whole procedure again.

Without doubt sweeping is a very effective way to fish wet flies. When you find a suitable stretch of river give it a try.

Let us now turn our attention to the expanse of flat water that follows on from the riffle we have just fished. Before we start fishing we must study the situation. There may well be fish in that flat area, but they will be off immediately if they catch a glimpse of us. A line landing on the water surface would also disturb them. If we are to be successful we must change our line; the floater we have been using on the riffle would cause a dreadful wake on that flat, slick surface. So before we even approach the flat area we must change our line to a slow sinker. The leader can stay the same, but we do not need a dropper fly and our point fly needs to be an imitative pattern, perhaps a gold-ribbed Hare's Ear.

Now for the approach. We must keep very low to ensure that we are in the blind area (see Figures 1 and 2, page 21), our movements must be slow, and we need to be in front of a neutral background. We must *not* wade, and we must *not* be on any skyline. It is best to quarter downstream (see Figure 10 on page 44). Sometimes such an area is fished upstream, in a similar way to the dry fly technique, but in that case takes are very difficult to detect.

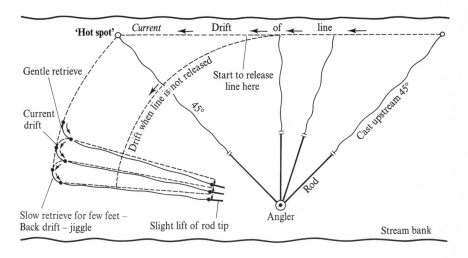

FIGURE 12   The standard upstream wet fly cast

This flat area might well produce the best fish of the day, but the results will depend on our tackle selection and on our very careful approach.

Chapter 6

Fishing Traditional Flies on a Small Stream

Today we will fish traditional wet flies on a small river (see Figure 13), and take advantage of two days of heavy rainfall, which should have made quite a difference to the state of the water.

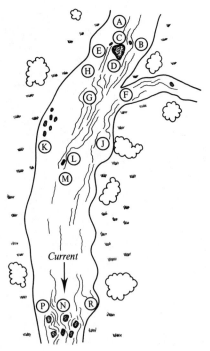

FIGURE 13   *Fishing a small river after rain*

Notice how coloured the water is – we cannot see the bottom anywhere – and it is much higher than expected. Small streams react to rain faster than larger rivers, but they usually clear down more quickly afterwards.

We will walk along the bank to point A, above the large protruding rock. The water must be up by at least 6 in (15 cm) – one can imagine what it must have been like immediately after the rain. The current is also very strong; we will have to be careful if we wade, as we will not be able to see where to put our feet.

It is not easy to clamber down the bank now that it is all mud. Pass the rod down first in case we stumble or slip – It is a fact of life that if one stumbles, one nearly always falls on the rod!

There is not much room to cast here, as we are too close to the bank and it is not possible to wade out into the main stream. However, as we are going to fish wet fly downstream, we will be able to roll-cast most of the time.

We will need to use a sinkant on our leader; a good one is a mixture of fuller's earth and washing-up liquid made up as a paste. It should not be applied to the whole leader, just the last 2 or 3 ft (60 cm–1 m). We will use a little on the fly as well, then give it a rinse.

What fly shall we use? Even though the water is a little coloured, we should still use a fairly drab traditional fly. We are fishing for brownies and they are not too partial to gaudy flies, even under these conditions. They are able to see in coloured water much better than one might think, and they will expect natural food to be brought down by the strong current. Something like a Lead-wing Coachman would be a good fly to start with.

We will strip a few yards of line off the reel and shake it out through the rod rings so that it floats downstream under our own bank – about 12 yd (11 m) is enough. While it straightens out in the current we can look things over and plan our strategy.

The fast water in the channel between the rock and the bank, at point B, looks particularly good, but we will fish this side of the rock first. Always fish the closer spots first so that you keep the disturbance to a minimum. We will cast to point C and let the current take the fly around this side of the rock to point

D. A roll-cast will do the job nicely. Knowing how to make a good roll-cast is half the battle on these small streams. You will find many places where a normal back-cast is impossible and a roll-cast is the only way to get the line out.

We have had no response so far. The next cast we will give a little action to the fly as it swims round the rock. We can do this by jiggling the line a little with the left hand and at the same time giving little jerks to the rod tip. The fly will then dart about as it swims downstream.

We must keep an eye on the upper part of the leader that is floating on the surface; a take as the fly travels downstream will rarely be felt on the line. If we see any unusual movement of the upper leader – a slight dip or a pause – then we strike. There is very little in a stream that will impede a wet fly swimming in the current, so any unusual movement is most likely to be a fish.

There is no response again. We will let the line continue on its way downstream and swing across in the current. As the line straightens out the fly rises to the surface in an arc. Unfortunately this is attractive to the smaller fish; sometimes they hook themselves, but mostly they only pluck at the fly. It is not always the small fry that do this, but we will soon know if it is a larger fish as the take is then very definite, and the fish is nearly always self-hooked.

I think the tendency of small fish to snatch at a rising fly is probably the reason why downstream fishing with a wet fly is not permitted on some rivers. I suppose one could use a much larger fly – say a size 10 or 8 – but I feel that a smaller hook, size 12 or 14, has much better holding power. A large hook is inclined to saw away and create a hole or tear out, resulting in damage to the fish. The smaller hooks dig in nicely. Of course, it is all relative to the size of the fish expected.

We will now cast over to that channel at point B. We will have to flip our line over the rock as soon as the cast is completed otherwise it will not be able to travel downstream. This is called mending the cast. We must remember to keep the fly working and to keep a sharp eye on the length of floating leader.

We have a fish! It is a good one too, playing deep – that is always a sign of a good-sized healthy fish. He is one for our bag.

I suggest we move downstream a bit to point E. I do not think we will get another fish out of that channel today. At point E we will be able to roll-cast to just above the mouth of the inlet at point F, then let our cast swing round in the current to point G. We will keep the cast short so that we do not disturb the undercut bank below the inlet; we want to fish there later.

The inlet is a minor torrent after all the rain and it is really churning up the main stream. I am sure the fly is not working deep enough; the current is keeping it too close to the surface. We really want it to be about 4 ft (1.2 m), deep, so we need a weighted fly.

I do not have a weighted Lead-wing Coachman, but a weighted Hare's Ear will do the job. It is a good all-round fly, especially in high water. Now the leader has all but disappeared. The fly is well down, just where we want it to be. We will keep it working with lots of little darting movements. Now it will make quite an arc as it heads for the surface below us.

A fish! I do not think he is big, as we have all the pull of the current against us as well as the fish. Bad luck, he got off! That is a shame, but the current is very strong and the odds favour the fish in these conditions. There is not much we can do about it except to tell ourselves that he could not have been very big!

Let us examine the fly. After a fish is lost in that manner, always have a good look at the fly. You never know, he may have got off because the barb was broken – it can break against a rock or stone – or he may have damaged the hook. In either case it would be useless to continue to use the same fly.

After that contact with a fish it would be better to move down-stream a little and cover some new water. We can move down to point H and have a go at the undercut bank at point J. From point H we can easily cast to point J, but we will have to overcome the fast centre current. Drag is not the problem, our difficulty is to get the fly down deep enough before it is swept away. With the water so high the hole will be quite deep, and any fish there are sure to be well down.

I will change the fly for something larger, less streamlined – something that will sink quickly. A weighted Woolly Worm will suit very nicely. Before we put it on we had better make an alter-ation to our leader. Although it is good practice to fish as fine as possible, there comes a time when common sense must prevail, and a fly that has the bulk and weight of a Woolly Worm needs a heavier tippet. We must make sure that we thoroughly soak the Woolly Worm, and at the same time apply sinkant to the leader.

There is no response the first time, although there was nothing wrong with our presentation, and I cannot believe there are no fish under the bank. Let us try it again. This time, we will cast a little further upstream so that the fly is swimming deeper by the time it is well into the eddy.

We have another fish! We must gain control quickly, as there is too much line out. He is not moving out, so perhaps we are snagged up. No, now he is moving away from the bank; he is a nice fish, and fighting well. He is certainly a wily character and knows his way around the stream. That undercut bank must be full of snags; the tree roots show even above the water-line. At one stage I was sure we had lost him, but now we have him.

If we now go down to point K, we may be able to wade out towards point L. Although the water is high, the stream bed is fairly level between K and L. As it happens we cannot wade out quite as far as point L. But we are still in a good position to fish the pool from point M to point N.

This type of water requires a rather special technique if one is to cover it properly. It is a wide, long area, without any real features, and the fish could be anywhere. The fast current upstream will bring plenty of food down and the comparatively slower water here will turn the whole area into a feeding ground. Under these conditions I suggest we employ the sweeping technique (see Chapter 5); it can be done with the minimum of casting and ensures that practically every foot of water is covered.

Before we start we will change the tippet back to thinner nylon and dry the whole leader with a piece of rag. Now we can grease the upper portion so that it will float, and treat the tippet portion with sinkant. We do not want to fish deep here – a couple of feet down will do nicely. We can use our Coachman fly again.

Having covered quite a lot of pool, I am surprised we have not taken a fish by now; we are working the sweep very well. Now we have one – a nice one too!

We will carry on sweeping, and we may catch another. Now is the time to be really attentive. We are starting to fish in the tail of the pool and that is always a gathering point for the fish. Any fish we take near points P, N or R will be dangerously close to these rocks and the fast water below. Once into the rocks and fast water, they will be lost to us.

We nearly had another fish but we have lost him. Nevertheless, it has been a good day. It will not do any good to fish in this pool until it settles down again, and that will take quite a time. Shall we call it a day?

Chapter 7

Nymph-type Flies

I refer to 'nymph-type' flies for a very good reason. Although there are accepted patterns for natural nymph imitations, there are not very many of them, and most so-called nymph patterns are really impressions of nymph-type creatures.

Nymphs

True nymphs basically belong to one of three orders of water-bred flies. Ephemeroptera (the up-winged mayfly types), Trichoptera (the sedges) and Plecoptera (the stone flies). The nymphs are the larvae of these flies and can be of four types: free swimmers, crawlers, burrowers or flats.

The free swimmers are a large group mostly belonging to the Ephemeroptera. They have a streamlined, elongated shape with a thorax that is as high as it is wide. Their speed through the water depends on the genus.

The flats also mostly belong to the order Ephemeroptera, but they can also be Plecoptera. In the main they are flat-bodied nymphs that are ideally adapted to movement among the stones and gravel. They are able to move quite fast when the need arises, but prefer to cling to stones and rocks. Their flat shape allows water to flow over them without dislodging their hold.

Crawling nymphs can also be Ephemeroptera or Plecoptera. They live among the silt, sand, gravel or stones found on the bottoms of rivers and stillwater. They are poor swimmers and very slow movers; their tails are covered in fine hairs and are of little use in propelling them through the water.

Burrowing nymphs are mayflies (*E. danica*), and live in small holes which they excavate in the mud or silt. They burrow by means of 'tusks' at the front of the head, called mandibles, assisted by very strong front legs.

The larvae of the Trichoptera could also be classed as burrowers, but in this case they build their own tunnels or cocoons out of silt and debris.

Nymph Patterns and Nymph Fishing

Nymph fishing was pioneered by the late G.E.M. Skues on the southern chalk-streams of the UK. His work was published in 1910. The controversy over the subject was enormous and the angling journals of the early twentieth century were filled with letters for and against the use of nymphs.

The dry fly purists of the day did not approve of nymph tactics, not even when the nymph was fished upstream in a similar manner to the dry fly. It was not only regarded as unsporting, it was clearly not the pursuit of gentlemen!

Today the nymph is 'legitimate'. It is even accepted on chalk-streams, where much work has been done to perfect the technique. A famous chalk-stream river keeper, the late Frank Sawyer, devised several imitative patterns that are still in general use today; in fact most modern nymph patterns are based on the Sawyer nymphs.

Of course, it is of little use fishing imitations of crawlers or the burrowers, likewise the stone-clinging flats and the encased sedge larvae are of limited use to the angler. Therefore most imitative nymph patterns follow the general outline of free swimmers (see Figure 4 on page 32).

As I have said, apart from standard nymph patterns there are many impressionistic patterns in use, mostly devised for still-water fishing. Gordon Fraser, a well-known Midlands flytier, has originated several such patterns mainly for use on the reservoirs.

It has always been thought that a true nymph imitation is most difficult to achieve. It is hard to believe that a trout, underwater in his own element, with the imitation clearly in view, cannot tell

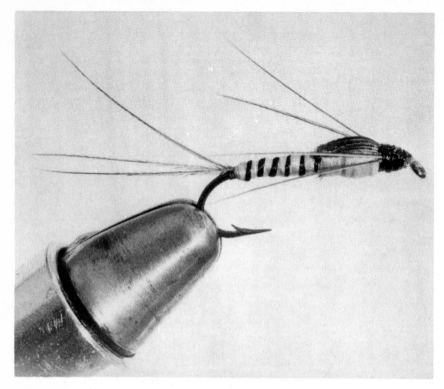

The Devastator Nymph.   A typical American pattern.

the difference. However, nymph imitative patterns *are* taken, and quite frequently.

The question has to be asked; if a nymph pattern is taken by the trout as a true nymph, does it not limit our chances? The nymph pattern can only imitate a nymph, whereas a traditional wet fly can be taken as a variety of foods (see Chapter 3). Are our chances not improved if we use a traditional wet fly instead of a nymph pattern?

The answer to this important question is very difficult. Research done by Ernest G. Schwiebert Jnr, which was published in 1955, found that rainbow trout take 85 per cent of their food subsurface, and brown trout 75 per cent. Schwiebert also found

56

that on average, an acre of river-bed concealed 100 lb (45.4 kg) of immature stream insects. A particularly rich stream had as much as 200 lb (90.8 kg) in the same area. Obviously trout have no difficulty in sustaining their subsurface feeding rate, and equally obviously a very large proportion of that feeding is on nymphs.

The problem that confronts the angler is that each time a trout takes a nymph the insect is probably behaving in a different way, sometimes being washed along by the current, sometimes darting from one weed bed to another, sometimes heading for the surface to hatch, etc.

A truly imitative nymph pattern, whilst ably representing a natural nymph, may not impart the correct impression when seen by the trout. It could well be that a traditional wet fly, being manipulated by the angler will give a much better impression. We have already seen that a traditional wet fly presents itself to a trout in a variety of ways, depending on the manipulation it is given, and the enormous success of these flies testifies to their effectiveness.

The difficulty in answering the question now becomes obvious. It is also now clear why effectively fishing an imitative nymph pattern is so demanding, probably the most demanding of all the flyfishing disciplines.

Of course, this does not apply in the same way to an impressionistic nymph pattern. Such a pattern is rather like another form of attractor wet fly, and is often very successful.

A nymph pattern that has received wide acceptance is my own Reflector Nymph. It was never really designed; it owes its origin to some obscure fly – I cannot remember which – that was in my fly box when I needed a fly with a gold-tinselled body for use in coloured water. Much later I formed the opinion that such a fly, having good reflective qualities, might well reflect the rocks and stones of the stream-bed when fished in clear water. In this way the light brown/amber translucence of the natural nymph might be imitated. It seemed a natural progression to clip back the regular wing so that the outline more closely resembled the natural nymph's wing cases.

Then, having little faith that it truly imitated any natural

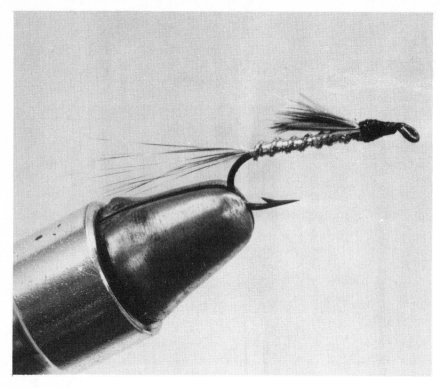

The Reflector Nymph

nymph, I relegated it to a corner of my fly box. But when I started using the sweeping technique, with the emphasis on the rising wet fly, I looked again at the fly with the gold-tinselled body. I tied more flies, this time with the body also ribbed with oval gold tinsel for increased reflection. In addition the finished bodies were treated to several coats of clear cellulose lacquer. As the intention was to create a nymph-like outline, I retained the clipped-back wing and added a long tail.

I am still far from convinced that the fly is a good nymph imitation, but I feel reasonably sure that the reflective qualities do give off a brown/amber translucence that is not out of keeping with natural insects. The clipped wing and long tail may or may not complete the illusion.

58

The results, however, have been excellent. Wild brownies, which are not usually inclined towards bright flies, have shown little hesitation in taking this fly, even in clear water. It is now one of the flies that I regularly use, and is my first choice for sweeping a pool.

There are several points that should be borne in mind when fishing nymph patterns. Most important, remember that although a natural nymph may be a free swimmer, it is still small and its movements are relative to its size. Natural nymphs do not dash through the water for several feet at a time at high speed. A short dash of a few inches is more natural, and all that needs is a jiggle of the flyline. Remember too, that the trout's approach is to a relatively slow-moving food morsel that does not have the ability to dash away. The take will therefore generally be slow and deliberate.

Such a take is very hard to detect and it may well be necessary to use some sort of bite indicator, particularly if you are fishing upstream.

Chapter 8

Nymphing on Stillwater

Today we will fish nymphs on the small stillwater where we fished previously (see Figure 5 on page 35). The fact that we have fished there before, and are familiar with the water, will be of considerable help to us.

Nymph fishing on stillwater is a very different proposition from nymphing on running water. I suppose it could be fairly said that it is akin to fishing a traditional wet fly, except that it is an attempt to simulate a variety of the smaller living organisms often found in stillwater. In other words, the name 'nymph' is somewhat of a misnomer as far as stillwater is concerned, for the intention is to simulate a wide range of pond life, including true nymphs, corixa, chompers, water boatmen, water beetles (both great and small), bloodworms, buzzers and pupae.

You might well ask, 'Why not fish a traditional wet fly or lure?' The answer lies in the satisfaction of successfully deceiving a fastidious trout that might not have taken a traditional wet fly or lure.

Because the intention is to simulate a wide range of underwater creatures, stillwater nymphs are mostly of the impressionistic variety. But, of course, there are many true nymphs in stillwater (pond olives, sedges, damselflies, dragonflies etc.), and a good imitative pattern will quite often outfish all others.

Nearly all the small stillwater creatures I have mentioned are to be found in water that is less than 15 ft (4.6 m) deep, and usually in the vicinity of weed beds.

Let us make a start by fishing the shallow end of the lake (see Figure 5, A to B). So far, we have not seen any flies (pond olives

60

or sedges) on the water surface, only a few damselflies dancing over the water. So let us begin over by the weed bed, where the water is approximately 4–6 ft (1.2–1.8 m) deep. We will use our usual technique and tackle up to make our first few casts well back from the bank (see Chapter 5).

As there are a few damselflies about it would be a good idea to start off with an imitative damselfly nymph. The natural nymph is a voracious little predator that lurks in weed beds and darts out to take its prey, which could be any one of a multitude of tiny underwater creatures. The trout know this routine only too well and patrol near the weed beds on the lookout for these nymphs.

We will use a floating line and make our first cast to the near edge of the weed bed. We must stay back from the bank, and at the same time keep very low. A count of five will allow the nymph to sink just below the surface. Now we need a retrieve that will give the impression of a fast-darting nymph, so we will make a series of sharp 6–8 in (15–20 cm) pulls on the line. If we allow the nymph to rest for a few seconds between each pull, for a count of five, it will allow it to sink slowly ready for the next pull.

There is no result from our first cast, so we will keep retrieving until we are well clear of the weed bed. Our next cast must be to the opposite side; if we cast to alternate sides we will keep the disturbance to a minimum.

Having made quite a few casts round the weed bed without any success, there is suddenly a savage take. It is a nice fish, a rainbow of about 2 lb (900 g). When you fish a darting damselfly pattern, you must always be prepared for smash takes, as the trout hit the natural damsel nymph very fast and hard.

We have created such a disturbance landing the fish that it would be prudent to move to the opposite bank.

I had intended to continue with the damselfly pattern, but there are a few pond olives on the water. It's not much of a hatch, but it may develop. We might try a pond olive nymph just below the surface, as if it were on its way to the surface to hatch.

There is quite an open expanse of water between us and the area which is 6–8 ft (1.8–2.4 m) deep. Moreover, there is a cool wind on our backs, and that means a subsurface flow of warm water is coming towards us.

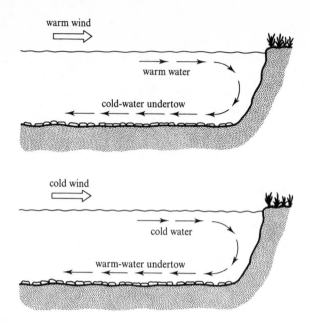

FIGURE 14   The effect of wind on stillwater

Let me explain. Generally speaking a wind will push the surface water (and the trout food) across the water in the direction in which it is blowing, i.e. to the windward shore. However, as the surface water meets the windward shore there is a tendency for it to be pushed down and return as an undertow back towards the lee shore. Consequently, as our wind is a cool one, pushing chilled surface water towards the opposite bank, the warm water below (and the trout food) will return in our direction in the form of this undertow (see Figure 14). So the pond olive nymphs are more likely to be hatching close to our bank before being blown further out across the water.

We will keep to our floating line but change over to a Pheasant Tail pattern which is a first-class imitation of a natural pond olive nymph. On some waters the pond olive nymph is more brown than amber/green, so if we get no response to our Pheasant Tail we will try a gold-ribbed Hare's Ear, which is a good

62

alternative. We will start by keeping well back from the bank and using the fan-casting technique (see Figure 6 on page 36), first, close by to the margins, then slowly increasing the length of our casts. We need to fish the nymph very close to the surface, a count of three should do the job very nicely.

Our pond olive nymph, the Pheasant Tail, is not in the same category as the damselfly nymph. The pond olive is a member of the order Ephemeroptera. As it rises to the surface to hatch, it floats at various levels, then hovers just below the surface film ready for metamorphosis. We require almost no movement of the nymph, just a very, very, slow hand-twist retrieve to keep the line straight so that a take can easily be detected. With the wind behind us the retrieve is almost unnecessary; it is an ideal situation.

Patience is the name of the game, and each cast has to be left in position for several minutes. At last our patience pays off, and we have a couple of nice plump rainbows to show for our efforts – which proves that an almost stationary nymph just under the surface can really produce results.

There have been no pond olives hatching for some little time now, and the fish also seem to have deserted us, so it would be a good idea to move our operations to area C.

Here we are confronted with much deeper water than we have just been fishing, and although a variety of pond olives hatch from deep water there is no sign of that happening today.

There is probably quite a thick weed cover over the lake bed, even though it does not extend to the surface and is not apparent to us. It would be a good idea to fish deep, but just above or through the weed cover. There are so many different pond creatures down there that we need an impressionistic pattern, a slow-moving fly that looks interesting enough to investigate, but at the same time could represent all manner of food items.

I suggest we use a weighted Stickfly, a very old pattern that is very similar to an even older one called a Wormfly. Flies that have a long proven record are always worth considering.

We will change to a slow-sinking line and use the count down system to find our fishing depth. We will know when we reach bottom as we will feel the weed cover when we start to retrieve.

We can then adjust the count so that we are retrieving just above the weed cover.

The main problem we will face is that the slow-sinking line continues to sink all the time it is in the water, and the weighted fly stays level with the line. Consequently, although our count down may be correct at the commencement of the retrieve, before very long we will be down in the weeds and possibly snagged.

Fortunately there is a technique to overcome this problem. When a line, leader and fly are drawn sharply through the water the water resistance causes them to rise towards the surface. Therefore if we abandon our slow hand-twist retrieve and manipulate the fly with short, sharp pulls, with a rest between each pull, we will be constantly rising above the weeds.

But let me be clear. I am not talking about the fast line stripping that is so often seen on stillwaters, where the line is retrieved at a rate much faster than the movement of any living creature. What I am suggesting is that we give short, sharp pulls of about 6 in (15 cm), then pause for a count of two before the next pull. This will give the impression of a darting creature that rises slightly each time it moves, then sinks slowly as it rests between each movement.

The most likely time for a take will be when the fly is stationary. Having seen the sharp movement, the fish will take the fly as it comes to rest. It is necessary to be prepared for this to happen just as we commence one of our sharp pulls. A fish pulling one way as we pull another is a sure recipe for a broken leader. I usually start my pulls very gingerly for a couple of inches, then finish them quite sharply when I am confident that a fish is not mouthing the fly.

Chapter 9

Nymphing on a River

On the river, one has to forget most of the stillwater nymph tactics, as they are not very helpful. River nymphing not only calls for a different technique; the whole concept is also entirely different.

We will fish the riffles and flats we visited before (see Chapter 5), beginning at the head of the riffles and using a 'downstream' approach.

It is important to choose the correct nymph pattern. We are not concerned with impressionistic patterns here, as we intend to imitate the natural nymph, and that means we have to decide which one to imitate. During the course of the fishing season various aquatic flies predominate at different times. Although there is no hard and fast rule (weather and temperature cause great variations), and the matter is complicated by some varieties which hatch on and off throughout the season, it is possible to formulate a general schedule.

As a general rule of thumb, we can say that large dark olives usually predominate early in season and again at the end (March/April and September/October). The iron blue is a poor-weather fly that is often to be seen during cold, overcast and windy days, mostly during May and June. Blue-winged olives are often to be seen from June onwards, and small olives often appear during July and August. Small spurwings hatch regularly during the height of the summer, as do pale wateries, and various sedges are out and about most days throughout the season.

It must be stressed that this list is nothing more than a very rough guide. Different waters, different localities, weather variations and varying water flows all combine to prevent it being entirely reliable.

When we fish the nymph, we have the advantage of not relying on fly hatches taking place at the time; natural nymphs are in the water at all times. But if we know when certain flies predominate it must influence our choice of pattern.

Today, being mid-season and the weather being good, we will use a small olive imitation, which usually means a Pheasant Tail. A sedge hatching pupae, (i.e. a Hare's Ear without the gold rib) would be a good alternative.

We will cast quartering across and downstream, (see Figure 10 on page 44), somewhat similar to the way we fish the traditional wet fly, but the follow-through after the cast is completed will be very different. On completing the cast we will lower the rod tip to water level and follow the nymph during the short free drift period, making sure we keep a straight line with very little slack. As the nymph swings round in the current we will continue to follow it, keeping the rod tip close to the water. On the completion of the swinging arc the nymph will, owing to the current, start to rise to the surface. We must now raise the rod tip to accelerate its rise, and then keep the rod high to retain it at the surface, often referred to as 'on the dangle'.

This technique, known as the Leisenring Lift, originated with two American flyfishers named James Leisenring and Pete Hidy. They co-authored a book entitled *The Art of Tying the Wet Fly and Fishing the Flymph* which was published in 1941 in the USA, then reissued in 1971. Many writers have advocated this procedure without giving due credit to the originators. Sometimes it is practised downstream, and at other times upstream, when it is often referred to as an 'induced take'. Leisenring and Hidy called their nymphs 'flymphs', which when you think about it describes the technique beautifully. (A method combining fly and nymph techniques.)

Once the nymph is at the surface it should be kept there on the dangle. Hopefully it will give the impression of a natural nymph at the surface, ready to hatch and swimming against the current. We should be in no hurry to spoil the effect; all the time we seem to do nothing we are still actively fishing.

We have not had any offers to our nymph, so we will move

downstream a few yards and repeat the process. We must be very alert for a take at three stages: immediately as the nymph swings across the current in a rising arc; as the nymph is hurried to the surface by the rod-lift; and on the dangle. The second stage is the most productive.

There is a splashy little rise downstream by a rock, if I had not been looking right at it, I would have missed it, rises are so fast in turbulent water that they are almost never seen. However, at least we know a fish is there, and it gives us a chance to use another form of the Leisenring Lift.

We will cast our nymph quartering downstream to a point that is about 6–8 ft (1.8–2.4 m) to the side of the fish's position. At the same time we will make sure that the cast is several feet short. The current will now take over and swing the nymph in an arc so that it passes in front of the fish. As it does so we will raise the rod tip in the Leisenring Lift.

Success! What a pretty way to take a fish!

I suggest we take a short rest then move over to the flats section of river. The commotion caused by that fish will have made further efforts here a waste of time for quite a while.

I think we should go below the flats so that we can fish upstream. We need to be below any fish to remain out of sight. In a flat area a traditional wet fly requires movement to attract fish, while a nymph pattern needs a slower, more deliberate approach, very similar to a dry fly. After all, that is what it is – a dry fly about to hatch.

Fishing a nymph upstream will produce far better results than the downstream method. The problem is that a very large proportion of the takes are never detected. They are hard to see or feel, and one never knows how many fish have been missed.

It is an education to watch a trout on feeding station taking nymphs. On one occasion a friend and I watched two large trout that were in a flat area between weed beds. They retained their position with the merest wave of the tail, moving slowly and deliberately to the right and left to gently intercept nymphs being brought to them by the current. As a nymph approached, a trout opened its mouth and expanded its gills, and water and nymph were gently sucked in. Anything inedible was just as easily expelled before the mouth was closed. How can such a take be detected by an angler possibly 10–12 yd (9–11 m) downstream? Quite a problem!

We can overcome this problem to a large extent in several ways. Many tackle shops sell bite detectors in various forms. The US companies, such as Orvis, have a wide variety of vividly coloured little floating indicators that can be attached to the leader and are very easily seen from quite a distance. Several UK companies are making fluorescent coloured floating 'dough' that can be moulded onto the leader. All of these indicators work on the principle that no matter how lightly a fish 'mouths' a nymph, there will be a slight movement of the leader that will register on the indicator.

I have used most of these innovations in the past with varying success, but I must confess to a thorough dislike of the technique. To me, it is somehow just not flyfishing. I am always left with the feeling that I am artificial bait-fishing under a float. This is a strictly personal view, but it spoils my fishing enjoyment.

So today we will use my method: a lightly-weighted Pheasant Tail, a greased leader (except for the last 12 in (30 cm)) and a very large bushy dry fly on a short dropper located about 24 in (60 cm) above the nymph. The dry fly I prefer is a white palmered Bi-visible, size 12. I suppose we could now be accused of fishing 'dry/wet' (if there is such a thing), but I find it preferable to an indicator device – of course, it is all in the mind! But you will see that the dry fly is an excellent indicator, as it tends to disappear completely when the nymph is mouthed by a fish.

Before we continue, however, I must make a personal confession: there have been a number of occasions when the fish I have taken have been on the dry fly indicator, not on the nymph!

Our approach on the flats is to fish the dry fly upstream in the traditional way, looking for the slightest abnormal movement of the Bi-visible. Any movement or hesitation, and we must strike firmly. We will also strike if we see a silver flash in the vicinity of the submerged nymph, regardless of whether or not anything was registered on the Bi-visible.

Chapter 10

Lures

The Origin and History of Lures

Lures have been used in various forms to catch fish for centuries. It is a matter of record that in ancient times the Macedonians used 'long flies' to catch 'speckled fish'!

During the first half of the nineteenth century, American pioneers moving westwards in their wagon trains found that the Indians used lures to catch fish. The Indian lures, used from time immemorial, consisted of bone hooks enhanced with feathers and bunches of hair.

In the UK salmon fishermen have been using large flies with exotic dressings for many years. However, these are not really within the scope of our discussion; they are something peculiar to traditional salmon fishing.

It is not until the turn of the century, about 1903, that we find the first record of lures being used in sport fishing for trout. Theodore Gordon, a famous American flyfisher of that period, reported in the angling press that he used small lures in the mountain streams of upper New York State. Gordon called his flies Bumblepuppies and designed a number of them. Many Bumblepuppy patterns are still in use today and are very successful takers of fish.

After Gordon's death in 1915 his Bumblepuppy patterns were described in *The Complete Fisherman; The Notes and Letters of Theodore Gordon* by John McDonald, published by Charles Scribner's Sons of New York. For interest the various dressings are shown in Figure 15.

Head	:	red or yellow chenille, or black varnished
Tag	:	silver tinsel or red silk
Tail	:	red feather (quill)
Butt	:	red or yellow chenille
Body	:	white chenille (dressed full)
Ribbing	:	flat silver tinsel
Throat	:	badger hackle
Wing	:	white hair, white swan each side
Shoulder	:	widgeon feather
Cheeks	:	jungle cock

FIGURE 15   The Bumblepuppy as dressed by Theodore Gordon

At the same time as Theodore Gordon was working on his Bumblepuppies, a Mr Scripture, a New York lawyer, was designing a range of flies that we know today as Streamers and Bucktails (see Figure 16). The terms are fairly loose. Basically any lure with a wing of feather material is referred to as a Streamer, while Bucktail refers to a lure that has a wing of hair (see Figure 17).

Typical Bucktail

Typical Streamer

FIGURE 16   Typical Bucktails and
Streamers

Matuka Style

Short Shank Hook

Optic Bucktail

FIGURE 17   Varieties of lure

Some lures have a wing which is made of a combination of materials, and no specific name has been given to such flies.

By 1910 Streamers and Bucktails were widely used in the USA, particularly in the state of Maine for land-locked salmon and brook trout. From this point on lure fishing became accepted practice throughout the USA.

In the UK the use of lures, although known, did not find favour until after World War II. It was the advent of reservoir fishing for stocked rainbows that brought the change. American lures

71

were found to be very effective and the angling press gave wide publicity to the American patterns. Even more patterns were designed by the UK reservoir anglers. Today the origin of lures is rarely thought about, and their use has been accepted as a standard technique.

The lure is basically an imitation bait-fish, and traditional Streamers and Bucktails were designed with this in mind. Although some modern lures are far removed from bait-fish imitations, they are still usually the size of a bait-fish (minnow), and they are probably taken in anger, curiosity or playfulness, being seen as an intrusion of the trout's space by another fish.

A fairly new type of lure has now made an appearance – the mini-lure. Traditional lures have always been on the large size, up to 4 in (10 cm) long, and tied on long-shank hooks that could well be between size 2 and 8. Mini-lures are really miniatures of the same flies tied on long-shank hooks that are probably size 12 or 14.

Some old British patterns, traditionally used as loch flies, could also be classified as very small lures. Flies such as Peter Ross, Bloody Butcher, and Alexandra were certainly designed as tiny fish-fry imitations. These flies are still in use today on the reservoirs, lakes and lochs.

Although traditional lures were constructed with natural materials such as feathers, hair and fur, and proved themselves in use, modern lures are often quite different. Synthetic fibres, plastic (mylar) tinsels, synthetic threads that glitter and fluorescent dyes have all been pressed into use. The main reasons for this evolution are not hard to find. Most synthetic materials are not expensive to produce and can be sold at a price that is highly competitive with natural materials. Most synthetics were designed and manufactured for purposes other than tying fishing flies; the flytying market is just a further sales outlet that has developed as natural materials become scarce. In fact some natural materials are no longer available, as they are on a protected list.

Since the original Streamer and Bucktail lures made their appearance little else has changed. The materials might have changed but the design format today is very similar to that of the original lures (see Figure 18).

Stinger (hook in wing)

Tandem (double hook)

Weedless (upside down)

Weedless (upside down)

FIGURE 18   Varieties of lure

However, one major design departure deserves mention. Early in the 1960s a New York banker named Keith C. Fulsher designed a series of mini-lures that he named the Thunder Creek Series. Fulsher's mini-lures were, in effect, reverse-tied Bucktails. The beauty of these flies is that they can easily be tied down to size 16 long-shank hooks, and truly imitate the smallest fish-fry. Figure 19 shows the construction of the Little Brown Trout Lure.

73

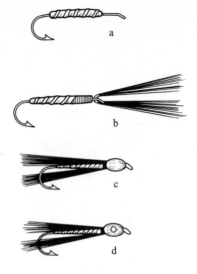

Body	:	Flat gold tinsel, ribbed with oval gold tinsel, well lacquered.
Upper wing	:	Coloured impala tail – a few strands of yellow, over which are a few strands of red, topped by a few strands of black.
Lower wing	:	A few strands of white impala tail.
Eye	:	Cellulose – large yellow, with black dot in centre.

FIGURE 19   *The Thunder Creek Little Brown Trout Lure*

Keith Fulsher was not the first to use this particular way of tying lures. Mrs Carrie Stevens, a noted Maine flytyer, had devised the method some years earlier for tying large Bucktails that were used for landlocked salmon. Keith Fulsher's contribution was the miniaturisation of the method so as to tie fish-fry imitations.

The Importance of Colour

As one walks along the bank of any reservoir, one is likely to hear the question, 'What colour did you catch that on?' Obviously practically all anglers appreciate that colour is very important, and that different colours seem to attract at various times. This is true, but there is a pattern to the attraction of different colours that is not so widely appreciated.

Two researchers, R.M.Ginetz and P.A.Larkin, thoroughly investigated the attraction of various colours in 1973. The results of their experiments, which totalled over 800, were published by the Institute of Animal Resource Ecology of the University of British Columbia, Canada. The details cover many pages, with numerous graphs and tables, but the following is a brief summary of their findings.

Experiments were carried out with rainbow trout that had been deprived of food for several days. Coloured, and multi-coloured, pellet food was then offered under different conditions of light and background. It was found that seven colours were particularly attractive; blue, red, black, orange, brown, yellow and green, not necessarily in that order, although blue was found to be highly acceptable under nearly all conditions.

Under poor light, against a dark background, the combinations of yellow and orange, and green and red were the most attractive. Under very low light, yellow was the first choice, while under high light, and in first-class visibility, red and blue were the most attractive. At all levels of light yellow attracted to other colours.

It was also found that certain combinations of colour were more attractive than others, namely yellow and black, yellow and blue, and red and orange.

It is obvious therefore that the acceptance by the fish of a certain colour is not a matter of pure chance, nor the mood of the fish. Light conditions and colour combinations are the factors that influence choice. We should select our colours according to the type of day (bright or overcast) and to the depth at which we are fishing (which affects light and visibility). It may even be a good idea to make out a list based on the above information, and keep it in the fly box.

Chapter 11

Lure Fishing on a Small Stream

Today we will fish a small stream I know well near the South Wales coast. It is the start of the season, so I am afraid that it is a very cold day, with a north-easterly wind which will not be much help. During the summer months the water in this stream is little better than a series of riffles between the deeper holes, but at this time of the year the flow will be much stronger and the holes deeper. It should give us a good opportunity to try out different tactics with mini-lures. I suggest we start with a size 14 fly in the Thunder Creek Series, a Little Brown Trout lure (see Chapter 10).

If you look at Figure 20, you will see that a small bridge crosses the stream. We will park the car near the bridge and start our operations from there.

To enjoy fishing on a day like this it is essential to be properly dressed, a day can be so easily spoiled by lack of forethought. Several layers of light clothing are much better than a heavy woollen sweater, and I find that a pair of thermal socks – at least knee length – are essential if you are intending to wade. It is a fact that if your head is cold you feel cold all over, so a warm hat is also necessary. A windproof fishing jacket will also help maintain body warmth. For years I have always used a pair of gameshooter's string mittens at this time of the year; they have non-slip palms and soak up very little water.

Before we commence fishing we will have to make changes to our leader to accommodate the mini-lure. We will add a 24 in (60 cm), length of 2x nylon as a tippet. Although the mini-lure is not particularly heavy, it is a larger fly and requires the heavy tippet to make it work properly through the water.

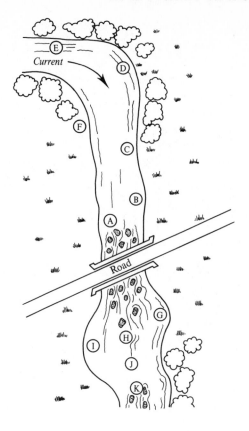

*FIGURE 20   Fishing a small stream with
                mini-lures*

The whole purpose in using the mini-lure is to fish the deeper holes and pools. It will be fished in the same manner as a bait-fisher uses a small minnow. The browns are now lean and hungry and are looking for something quite substantial.

Let us walk upstream along the bank to point E. There is a good hole at Point D that might hold a fish or two. The water at point E is not deep, so we will be able to wade quietly to give ourselves room to cast. You can see that the bend in the stream has created a minor pool with a deep hole under the far bank. There is a definite water flow but it is steady rather than fast. In this type of

A Thunder Creek style mini-lure.   See Figure 19 for tying details.

fishing we will ignore the direction of the current, except where it helps us to get the fly down to where the fish may be lying. Most of the larger fish are now deep, where the water is warmer.

When we fish a mini-lure it must never just be carried by the current, it must be constantly on the move, imitating a fish-fry. We must impart a constant darting action by manipulating the line with the left hand and at the same time moving the rod tip. It is a similar routine to the way we made traditional wet flies work, but this time we will also be retrieving across and against the current.

We will make our first cast, a short one, to just above point D. Now we start paying out line, stripping it from the reel and passing it through the rod rings by waggling the rod tip from side to side. As the current takes the fly downstream there will be movement caused by the waggling rod tip, and all the time it will be sinking deeper.

Now that the fly is in the pool we can start the retrieve by short, sharp pulls on the line. Every few pulls we make a pause to let the fly sink back with the current, then carry on as before. It is a 'sink and draw' type of retrieve that we are trying to achieve. We will also vary the length of the pulls, so that we get a nice darting action with a sink-back in between. When we have retrieved enough line we will be in a position to cast again.

If the fly needs to swim a little deeper we must delay the retrieve for a while, but keep the fly moving by jiggling the rod tip.

We will soon know if the fly is taken; we are trying to imitate the movements of a small bait-fish, and if we are successful the take will be a savage attack. Brown trout normally hit their prey at the head end, and hit very hard. An instantaneous strike back could well cause a break; on the other hand we will need to set the hook which may not have taken a good hold. Whenever I can, I try to exercise enough self-control just to tighten as soon as I feel a take, then a split second later I strike back to set the hook – much easier said than done!

Our next cast seems to be working out well, the fly is quite deep down in the pool, and we keep it working with short, sharp, pulls, moving the rod tip at the same time. We are into a fish! We must keep a tight line, and have the net ready. He's a nice-sized fish, but lean; he must have been really hungry. We will gently put him back and maybe catch him again later on in the season when he is in much better condition.

Although we normally think of the early season as the best time for this type of fishing, the mini-lure can be just as effective at other times. I well remember such an occasion. It was very early one morning, shortly after dawn, and I was fishing Wiskoy Creek in the USA. It was midsummer and the morning was beautiful and clear. My path down to the stream took me over a very old wooden bridge made up of planks that had seen better days – there were wide gaps between them. I looked down through the gaps into a deep pool beneath the bridge. The sides were of shelving rock that disappeared into the depths. Several large trout were lying quite deep along the rock, probably at least 6 ft (2 m) down.

I made my way upstream of the bridge and selected a mini-lure. I then used the same technique we have just been using, paying out line and letting the fly pass right under the bridge until it reached the other side. After a short pause to let the lure sink low in the water, I started an erratic retrieve.

You can imagine the shock I received when the water under the bridge suddenly seemed to explode. I am sure the spray must have reached the underside of the bridge. The fish I had hooked made a series of leaping jumps under the bridge, which were most difficult to control. After the most amazing fight I was able to net the fish out safely – a wild rainbow of over 2 lb (1 kg).

Let us now move downstream a little to point F. The opposite bank, from point C to point B is well undercut and quite deep. We can make a series of casts to that bank between the two points, then retrieve the fly back across the stream. The current will keep the line taut so all we have to concentrate on is a good erratic retrieve.

The first cast is not good; we were working it well enough, but the result is little different from using a traditional wet fly. We must remember at all times that we are trying to simulate the movements of a small fish-fry, so our retrieve must be faster and more erratic so as to overcome, and cut across, the current. We will try again.

The next attempt is a lot better. It does not matter if the lure is sometimes almost on the surface, just as long as it keeps darting about.

That bank did not produce anything for us, but it was a good place to try. Using these tactics we have to search every deep hole and undercut bank that we come across. A favourite lie of trout is often under a bridge if the water is deep enough (see Figure 21). In this case, however, there is no deep pool under the bridge, just white water over the pile of rocks. The deep pools are downstream the other side. Now that we are near the bridge let us go back to the car for some hot coffee; afterwards we can fish the pools below the bridge.

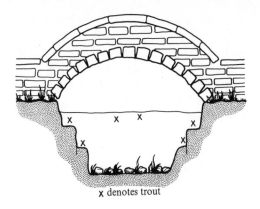

x denotes trout

FIGURE 21   A bridge lie

If you look below the bridge you will see that the stream opens out. The rocks under the bridge have created a miniature waterfall at point A, but at point I it is quite shallow, and the centre current between points H and J has scoured out a deep channel. I have been here in the summer when the water was considerably lower and it was deep even then. The side eddy at point G is even deeper. It is almost still water, and it is a very interesting part of the stream.

I suggest that from point I we cast across the current to point J, then retrieve back through the tail of the fast water. I do not think we will pick up a fish in the fast water, but it would be wrong to ignore the area in front of us just because the eddy is more attractive and tempting. We can fish that afterwards.

We make two good casts, with the fly skipping through the fast water. It is very hard to make the fly swim deep through the current, for if we delay the retrieve the fly will only swing down below us into the shallow water. We will make our next cast right into the tail of the fast water, and then bring the fly back quickly with a series of sharp pulls, so that the fly plays just below the surface.

We have another fish! What a shame it is so small; we will handle it very gently and slide it back in the water. It is hard to believe that such a small fish would take a mini-lure; if it had really been a fish-fry he could never have swallowed it. I wonder what they think when they take food that size. Perhaps they do not think at all; it may be a matter of pure aggressive instinct.

Why are we using a mini-lure instead of wet flies? It is not easy to answer in a few words, but I will tell you about an incident that will explain the reasoning.

It was very early in the season, with the usual cold, unsettled weather, and a friend and I decided to fish a stream that flowed into a small lake. There was a small wooden bridge supported on sunken wood pylons that spanned the stream as it flowed into the lake. Standing on the bridge I could see a number of good-sized trout, at least six or seven, lying in a group among the sunken pylons. At first sight they appeared to be dormant, but small movements indicated that this was not so.

I called out to my companion on the bank and told him the position of the trout below me. While I looked down to watch the results, he cast a traditional wet fly between the pylons and retrieved it with a series of darting movements. The fly passed alongside the trout but brought no results. The trout certainly saw it – a couple of them even moved slightly away from it – but no attempt was made to take it or even to follow it. He made several casts, but the result was the same each time.

I then suggested that he change to a small lure. As soon as the lure was cast and retrieved through the pylons, several fish turned towards it. Before it had moved very far it was hit quite savagely by one of the larger fish.

It is not possible to reach a firm conclusion as to why the lure worked, but I believe that early-season trout are not very interested in flies that simulate food that is not yet available to them. During the very early season there is a decided lack of underwater insect activity, and I do not think the trout are expecting such food, or even looking for it. I also believe that because of their generally poor condition, they are not inclined to hunt small morsels of food until the supply is adequate and worth the energy expended.

The mini-lure may be taken for two reasons. Obviously it represents a more substantial piece of food that may be worth the effort needed to secure it, but I do not think that is the whole story. There is the very real probability that the trout resent any invasion by small fry as a threat to their future food supply. In their early-season condition they do not want to have to compete for food with eager young fry; consequently, they automatically attack any intrusion into their space. So we use a mini-lure to search out those deeper areas where the larger fish choose to lie pending their return to top condition. It is an invasion of their privacy, and we hope it will receive the full treatment in response!

Let us now try a cast to the eddy at point G. It looks a very good spot for a fish and it is certainly deep enough. We will cast slightly upstream into the rough water just above point H, then let the current take the fly into the eddy. We must wait for the fly to sink as deep as possible before it begins to leave the eddy. I would like to think that we could place the fly right on the bottom before we retrieve it to the surface.

Having given it enough time, we will now move the fly as fast as possible, with a retrieve of short, sharp pulls, fast and erratic, right up to the surface and out of the eddy.

Another fish! We must keep a tight line on him. He does not have anywhere to go, but look at the rod bend! He is a good one; we must have taken him just as the fly lifted off the bottom. He is deeper than we thought, but he is coming up now. We will lead him below the fast water. He is finished now, and safely in. It is the best fish I have seen from this water, but see how lean he is? In three months time he will be well over 1½ lb (700 g). We will put him back and let him have a few months to put on weight.

Chapter 12

Lure Fishing on Stillwater

Today we are going to use full-sized lures on stillwater.

Most lure fishing takes place on reservoirs, but it would be impossible to cover reservoir fishing in any detail in a book of this nature. Both boat and bank fishing are specialised activities, and whole books have been written on both techniques. Never-the-less many of the anglers you see fishing from the banks of a reservoir are working pretty much on a 'chuck and chance it' basis.

So if you want to know more about reservoir techniques, I would suggest that you read about them in the specialised books that are available. In the meantime, we will return to our small private stillwater (see Figure 5 on page 35), and hopefully lay a foundation that will stand us in good stead for lure fishing elsewhere on larger waters.

Let us approach the water in our usual way (see Chapter 5), and tackle up well back from the water's edge. While we are putting our tackle together we can take stock of the weather and light conditions, and formulate our plan of action.

We know that we first have to find the swimming and feeding level of the fish, then, according to prevailing light conditions at that depth, decide on an appropriate colour or colours, for the lure.

As it is an overcast day, and a trifle on the cold side, we can make a start by assuming that the fish will be well down. Light conditions are poor, and will be even poorer at depth, so we will need a lure with yellow or a yellow/black combination in the pattern (see Chapter 10).

I suggest we fish area C, where we have a greater depth of water, and use an Edson Light Tiger lure (see Appendix C). A slow-sinking line and the counting down technique will help us start on the bottom, and we can then vary the count so that we will systematically fish all depths up to the surface. It should not take us very long to establish the swimming depth of the fish.

We will fan-cast the area, and use a fairly fast retrieve of long, steady pulls. Remember, we are not imitating natural food, we are trying to arouse a reaction of curiosity, playfulness or anger at the intrusion.

We get our first serious pluck at the lure when we are retrieving about 3 ft (1 m), off the bottom, i.e. at about 9 ft (3 m) deep. We were right about the fish being well down, and at that depth the visibility will be very poor. We missed the fish, but we have now learned what we needed to know. If we do not get results with the Edson Light Tiger, we will change to another low-visibility lure, in red and orange, such as a Micky Finn (see Appendix C).

Our systematic approach has paid off – we caught nothing on the Edson Light Tiger, but we have two very nice fish taken on the Micky Finn.

As things have now become very quiet let us move to the other side of the little dam. The water is still about the same depth and it will give us the opportunity to try a different technique.

I am going to use an all black Woolly Bugger (see Appendix C) and fish it right on the bottom. In a way this will be an imitative lure, as I hope to simulate the movements of a black leech. Although black is not one of the most attractive colours in poor light, in this instance we are not trying to induce a non-feeding response. Fish are able to find food items at considerable depths, partly by sight and partly by picking up small vibrations on the nerve system along their lateral line.

We are not really retrieving the Woolly Bugger at all, just giving a series of quick tweaks in between varying periods of rest. And after only a few minutes, we have another nice fish on the bank – better than either of the other two.

I once had an experience that taught me a great deal about fishing the Woolly Bugger. A friend and I were fishing a small stillwater in upper New York State during the summer months, when the water was low and very clear. My friend was using a large, size 6, Woolly Bugger, and I could clearly see it inching its way over the bottom. I was suddenly startled to see a very large rainbow of at least 8 lb (3.6 kg) appear from under the bank and pick it up. I immediately realised that the fish was swimming *towards* my friend, who was completely unaware of what had happened. 'Strike!' I yelled.

'Why?' he called back. I tried to splutter an explanation, but I was too late. The Woolly Bugger was back on the bottom and the fish had gone. My friend never did believe my story; I wonder how many fish we miss without knowing anything about it.

Chapter 13

The Booby

The combination of new flytying materials and very fast-sinking lines has enabled the angler to fish a lure right on the bottom of quite deep water. Lures such as Dog Nobblers, Tin Heads, Lead Heads, Gold Heads and Chainbead Heads have been developed to achieve this deep fishing ability. These patterns are often effective, and they are interesting to tie, but the fishing technique was pretty well covered in Chapter 12, when we dealt with the Woolly Bugger, and no further explanation is really necessary. The patterns themselves are easily obtained from most pattern books or writings on stillwater and reservoir fishing, and various flyfishing mail-order catalogues also list and illustrate the various lures and the beads necessary to dress them.

However, there is one type of modern bead-headed lure that is probably the most important of the new innovations: the Booby. It is in a class of its own. The reason for the name will become evident when you see the way the beads are tied in.

The Booby, or Booby-nymph as it is often called, is a bead-headed fly with a difference. The beads are not solid, so they do not weigh enough to sink the fly. They are made of high-density plastazote (ethafoam), and are intended to give the fly extreme buoyancy, yet interestingly, the Booby technique still calls for the fly to be fished deep on the bottom. See Figure 22 for instructions on tying a Booby.

The Booby was the brainchild of Gordon Fraser, a well-known Midlands professional flytyer. He has made it clear that the idea of using ethafoam beads was not his; it probably originated in the USA. But the form and the fishing technique are his.

It is not a specific fly; the name really refers to a type of

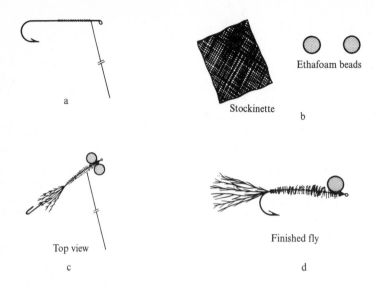

Ethafoam beads

Stockinette

Top view

Finished fly

a Lay a base of thread to the hook-shank.
b Prepare the stockinette and ethafoam beads.
c Wrap the beads in stockinette and stretch tightly. Bind them down onto the hook-shank then trim off excess stockinette.
d Finish the fly by adding the tail and dubbed body. The rib is optional.

Figure 22 Booby construction

construction. Many dressings and materials are used, and the fly is seen in a variety of colours. However, it is generally accepted that it has a large marabou tail, a dubbed body and perhaps a metallic ribbing of one sort or another. I have found that the brighter colours of red, orange and yellow dubbing, with a marabou tail of the same colours, seem to be the most attractive to the fish, perhaps because deep in the water, where visibility is poor, these colours are most easily seen by the fish (see Chapter 10).

It is impossible to say with any degree of certainty what the Booby represents to the fish. If we consider the comments on trout reactions in Chapter 2, we may well come to the conclusion that it might not be taken as a food. There is a possibility that the trout's reaction may be one of pure aggression, or just plain curiosity or playfulness. Aggression is strongly suspected as the Booby is often savagely taken by the fish on the run.

An incident that took place on a small private lake bears this out. I was having a lean time as far as results were concerned; the day was sunny and bright, with the fish well down and inclined to be inactive. So I decided to fish a Booby. Once it was cast out it became a waiting game. After giving plenty of time for the fast-sinking line to settle on the bottom, an occasional twitch was all that was required to keep the Booby bobbing, weaving and swaying about in the undertow. The line was not trapped by my rod hand, but was held loosely in my left hand directly from the rod's first ring.

After only a short while the line was pulled firmly through the fingers of my left hand. It was not the jerk or pull of a take, but a long, steady pull of a length of line. In all about 1 yd (1 m) of line passed through the fingers of my left hand before I arrested the run by lifting into the fish. In other words, the fish had attacked the Booby and taken it on the run, a fast and savage run, and had made no attempt to drop it when the resistance of the sunken line was felt.

Since very few food forms are taken in such a manner, one is left with the conclusion that the take was purely an aggressive act. For the record, the Booby was dressed with an orange marabou tail, an orange seal-fur dubbed body and gold wire ribbing. With the white ethafoam beads at the head it was quite a garish concoction.

The very nature of the Booby limits its use mainly to still-waters, except, perhaps, for those rare areas of rivers where the water is extremely deep and the current almost non-existent.

Chapter 14

Fishing the Booby

As I have said, it is just possible under the right circumstances to use a Booby-type lure on running water. But the right circumstances are very rare, as not many trout streams have sections that are not only deep but also almost devoid of current. Depth is necessary to use a Booby set-up effectively, and almost stillwater conditions are required for the correct manipulation of the lure. Consequently, the Booby is generally looked upon as a modern stillwater lure.

Today we will return to our favourite small stillwater (see Figure 5 on page 35). We can try our Booby technique in the deeper water, close to the dam, provided that conditions are favourable and the fish are low in the water.

Although the weather is fine and the sun quite bright, there is quite a nip in the air. Very early in the season there are often days like this. It is a pleasure to be out and about, but the water looks dead; no fish are showing and there is no apparent insect life to bring them to the surface. It can be safely assumed that most fish are very close to the bottom – definitely a Booby day!

During the early season I prefer to use the short Booby tackle-rig (see Figure 23). Later in the season the set-up shown in Figure 24 is more productive when buzzers are rising to the surface to hatch. It is at buzzer time that this rig, with a couple of buzzers on droppers, becomes a deadly way to take trout.

Today, the set-up without droppers can be very short indeed. During early season the weed growth on the bottom is not very prolific·and the Booby is only required to work a few inches above the weeds. A leader of 3–4 ft, (about 1 m) will be quite sufficient.

We will use a single strand of level nylon as a leader. There is

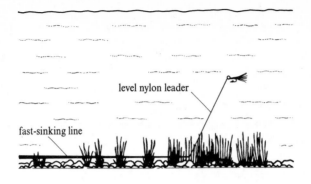

FIGURE 23   Short Booby tackle-rig

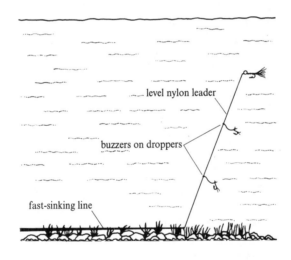

FIGURE 24   Booby tackle-rig with droppers

no need for it to be tapered, and about 5x (.006 in/.15 mm), will let the Booby operate completely unhindered. If we use double-strength nylon we will have a nylon strength of approx 3½ lb (1.5 kg). Casting will not be difficult as the Booby is very light and the leader very short.

Since the fast-sinking line has not been used since last season, we should draw off about 15 yd (13.5 m), and lightly stretch it between the hands to remove any tendency to coil. After long storage on a reel even a top-quality line will often develop coils. Today is on the cold side, and the water is decidedly cold, and any coils in the line will persist all day unless cured.

It is also a good idea, while we have some of the line off the reel, to rub a rag soaked in muddy water along its length. These preliminaries take up valuable fishing time, but they are well worth it once fishing commences. Nothing is more exasperating than struggling all day with a line in coils that simply refuses to sink evenly along its length.

The preliminaries over we can select our Booby. I suggest we use one that is either entirely yellow or at least has a yellow tail. Orange is better reserved for warmer summer days when large clouds of daphnia are moving through the water.

Once the cast is made we need to allow plenty of time for the line to sink and to settle evenly along the bottom. Patience is needed; very often two or three minutes is hardly enough time to be sure that the line and the Booby have settled into the correct position.

A word of warning. Although we are not actually doing anything while the rig is settling to the bottom, we need to be extremely vigilant, as the Booby is actually 'fishing' from the time it enters the water. Some time ago I watched an angler cast out a Booby then lay his rod down on the grass while he smoked a cigarette. He then went on to have a leisurely coffee from his thermos. If he had encountered a fish similar to the one described in the last chapter, he would have had to take a swim in the lake to recover his rod!

We will make sure we take a little more care. The rod can be laid down if you wish, but hold the line loosely in your fingers so that a take can instantly be detected.

When enough time has elapsed for the rig to have settled in position, give a tweak to the Booby by giving a short, sharp pull on the line. Deep down, the Booby, floating above the line and swaying in the undertow, will suddenly bob down, then float upwards again. What an enticing action! After a short pause, give the line a steady draw to make the Booby swoop downwards. Follow this with a series of tweaks.

I did say the take could be savage, and it is! We have a fish firmly on. Let him run. Now he is under control, and at last the net is under him – a nice fish, at least 3 lb (1.4 kg).

We now need to take a good look at the Booby, as the sharp teeth of a fish very often tear the nylon stockinette that encases the ethafoam beads. A Booby is not the most robust of lures and fly wastage is on the high side. A couple of seasons ago I started tying Boobies using a thin square of polythene, to cover the ethafoam beads before stretching the stockinette over them. Not only does this construction make the fly more robust, it also keeps muddy water out of the beads, thus improving buoyancy.

There is no doubt that the Booby will take deep-lying fish when other methods fail. However, we must use some discretion in its use. When fish are cruising just below the surface or feeding from the surface insect activity, the Booby should stay in the flybox.

The art of taking fish is to understand which is the most productive technique in the given circumstances, which fly or lure best suits the technique being used, which colour the circumstances dictate, and what will be the possible reaction of the fish to our efforts.

Chapter 15

Weather and Conditions

I am not in any way, an expert on the weather, so I hesitated before writing this section. However, knowing how much my fishing has been influenced by the weather, it would be very remiss of me not to pass on the observations I have made over the years.

Temperature

Temperature has an effect on trout, but only at times of extreme heat and cold is it really noticeable. I have taken good fish when the weather has been much too cold to fish in comfort, particularly rainbow trout and brook trout. I have even taken good bags of them when there has been snow on the banks and slush floating in the stream. The brown trout is very sluggish at these temperatures, but will still feed to a certain extent.

A very high temperature is a different matter; trout become dormant very quickly as the temperature of the water rises and the oxygen content is depleted. I am now convinced that a sustained high temperature will destroy the fishing much more quickly than a severe cold spell. But of course, it all depends on the normal conditions; what is a high or low temperature to a fish in Alaska is totally different from that experienced by a fish in the UK. The normal conditions must be taken into account when calculating what effect a very hot or very cold temperature will have.

It must also be recognised that the temperature of running water is not influenced by isolated hot or cold days to the same extent as that of stillwater. Even a few consecutive days of

extreme temperature will seldom influence the stream temperature to any marked degree. The main problem with stream
fishing on a very hot day may well be the very bright sun; trout
do not like this brightness and will seek shelter from it.

Wind

Wind has a decided influence on our sport, but I have always
noted that its effect is very closely tied in with the atmospheric
pressure. As a small boy, fishing for roach with maggots, I was
taught the following traditional jingle:

> When the wind is in the east,
> Then the fishes bite the least;
> When the wind is in the west,
> Then the fishes bite the best;
> When the wind is in the north,
> Then the fishes don't come forth;
> When the wind is in the south,
> It blows the bait in the fishes mouth.

Is there any truth in it? Quite possibly. Trout do not like an
approaching low-pressure system – they feed more consistently
when the approaching system is of high pressure. In the UK most
low-pressure systems seem to come from the north and east, so
south or west winds may well offer an advantage. I was once told
that the prevailing wind over the UK was south-westerly, it
never seems that way to me!

You will have noticed that I talk about *approaching* weather
systems. I believe that the approaching system is far more important than the one that is already with us. While we are enjoying
a high-pressure weather system, trout will very often go off the
feed for no apparent reason, but it often transpires that the good
weather is fast coming to an end and a low-pressure system is
forecast. Trout are very sensitive to such a change, and often
react several hours before the change actually takes place. For
consistent feeding the pressure system needs to be settled for at
least forty-eight hours.

Sunshine

I am sure that trout are very sensitive to very bright sun, for a number of reasons. Their constant awareness of danger must be foremost. Looking into a bright sky, their vision is impaired, and consequently approaching danger may not be seen in time. Their eyes are also extremely sensitive to light; any creature that can see well in the dark – and a trout most certainly can – does not enjoy bright conditions. So when you are fishing on a beautiful, bright, cloudless summer day, look for trout in the shadier portions of the stream.

Rain and Mist

Rain has varying effects on the fishing; as with wind, it depends almost entirely on the atmospheric pressure. Rain itself is possibly beneficial, as it improves the oxygen content of the water and may consequently stir the fish into feeding activity. So if you like fishing in the rain – as I do – and the approaching weather system is not a low, you may well enjoy very good sport.

Small streams will usually begin to colour quite quickly if the rain is prolonged. I have found that the start of such coloration has served me very well. The trout seem to sense that additional food is on its way into the stream and usually commence their feeding activities. Once the water is highly coloured, however, fishing the fly is not very effective; the little boys with their worms will have much better results. High-spate water conditions usually bring on an extended feeding spell, and providing the water is not too coloured, good sport can be expected.

Very often when I have been fishing at dusk, and more particularly when I have been out shortly after dawn, I have met with the peculiar phenomenon of thick mist blanketing the water. This mist usually lies only inches deep while the air above is perfectly clear. Obviously this is caused by a sudden severe difference between the water and air temperatures. At dusk it has always created difficulties for me, as the fish seem suddenly to disappear. But whenever I have encountered it at dawn it has been a different story; the sport has been terrific. I cannot understand the reason for this difference; I mention it simply as an observation that may be of use to others.

I think that the effect of thunderstorms on trout are a mystery to us all. At times trout will feed avidly just before, during or just after a storm. At other times it is the complete reverse. There does not appear to be any set pattern. Few anglers will want to fish during a thunder storm, and it is probably dangerous to do so, but from time to time we are all caught out by such storms, and if we continue to fish, the results are completely unpredictable.

One such occasion happened in the Catskill Mountains. I was staying at a fishing lodge that had been built on the banks of the Beaverkill River. The front porch and lawn were only a few yards from the water's edge, and it was tempting to fish at odd times of the day and night. I had decided to do a little night fishing, and during the afternoon had mapped out several safe wading patterns. After a relaxed dinner I made my way across the lawn to the water. It had been a beautiful dusk and the night was clear and balmy. I commenced operations with a big, well-dressed fly. I could not see too well but kept in sufficient contact to have a fair idea of what was happening.

After a short while I could see fellow anglers taking their after-dinner coffee on the covered porch of the lodge, which was very well lit. The light also helped me in my fishing. Suddenly the sky lit up with lightning, then more lightning. Then came the rain – a real deluge. Within a space of a few minutes the lodge became just a glow through a sheet of falling water. I was wearing a loose fishing jacket and hat that were totally inadequate for the situation. I decided to stop fishing as fast as I could. At that precise moment I had a solid take to my fly, so definite that I felt a savage tugging on the line. I had no alternative but to stand there in the deluge and play the fish out.

It was a beautiful brownie, about 1½ lb (680 g), and it fought very hard. The darkness and rain made it impossible to use a landing net, so I ended the tussle by scooping him up in the hem of my fishing jacket! With the fish under my arm I made my way towards the lights of the lodge. I can just imagine the apparition I must have presented to those sitting and having coffee on the porch. Do fish feed during a thunderstorm? Sometimes, but trying to catch them in the process is not recommended!

Not all anglers can pick and choose the days they go fishing, and one must accept whatever weather presents itself when the opportunity to fish comes along. What I have said here may be of some help in indicating the quality of sport that might be expected, but weather is a most peculiar thing, and the trout are not always predictable. So if you have the chance to go fishing then go, and take your chances. A day spent fishing is never a waste of time, even if you do not catch any fish. We learn something every time we are on the water, and it is that store of knowledge that brings future success.

Appendix A
Wet Fly Patterns

Wet fly patterns

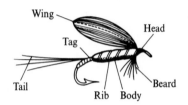

Alder

An old English pattern that has become very popular in the USA.
Hook: 12 or 14 wet fly
Tag : Flat gold tinsel
Body: Wound peacock herl
Wing: Brown turkey
Beard: Black hackle

Eric's Beetle

An English pattern that is really a sunken terrestrial.
Hook: 14 or 16 wet fly
Tag : Yellow wool
Body: Wound peacock herl
Hackle: A black hackle on the long side tied as a collar

Coachman

Often called a Leadwing Coachman. Old UK pattern.
Hook: 12 or 14 wet fly
Tag : Flat gold tinsel
Body: Wound peacock herl
Wing: Leaden-grey quill
Beard: Brown hackle

Royal Coachman

Probably the best-known pattern in the world. A very old UK fly.
Hook: 12, 14 or 16 wet fly
Tail: Golden pheasant tippets
Body: Wound peacock herl, in the centre a band of red silk so as to divide the body into three parts

Wing: White swan quill
Beard: Brown hackle

Peter Ross

An old loch fly that is effective for reservoir rainbows.
Hook: 8, 10 12 or 14 wet fly
Tail: Golden pheasant tippets
Tag : Flat silver tinsel
Body: Red fur (seal)
Rib : Oval silver tinsel, also wound over the tag
Wing: Teal
Beard: Black hackle

Partridge and Orange

A popular northern fly.
Hook: 12, 14 or 16 wet fly
Body: Orange silk
Hackle: Grey partridge wound as a collar sloping backwards

Snipe and Purple

Another popular northern fly that is said to imitate the Iron Blue drowned spinner.
Hook: 12, 14 or 16 wet fly
Body: Purple silk
Hackle: Snipe wound as a collar sloping backwards

March Brown

A wet fly that is popular on both sides of the Atlantic.
Hook: 12 or 14 wet fly

Tail: Brown partridge
Body: Dubbed hare's ear
Rib : Flat gold tinsel
Wing: Brown turkey
Beard: Brown partridge

Zulu

A pattern equally popular on both sides of the Atlantic. A good pattern for rainbows.
Hook: 10, 12 or 14 long
Tail: Tuft of red wool
Body: Black chenille
Rib : Flat silver tinsel
Hackle: Black tied palmer

Soldier Palmer

An old loch pattern.
Hook: 10, 12 or 14 long
Tail: Tuft of red wool
Body: Red fur (seal)
Rib : Oval silver tinsel
Hackle: Brown tied palmer

Bumble

Very old pattern that can be tied several ways.
Hook: 10, 12 or 14 long
Tail: Golden pheasant crest
Body: Black fur (seal)
Hackle: Black tied palmer, with a blue hackle at the front as a collar

Bloody Butcher

Called a Butcher because the inventor was a butcher by trade. A good fly for both river and still-water.
Hook: 12 or 14 wet fly
Tail: Slip of red quill
Body: Flat silver tinsel
Rib : Oval silver tinsel
Wing: Black quill
Beard: Black hackle

Gold Butcher

A good variation of the Bloody Butcher.
Hook: 12 or 14 wet fly
Tail: Slip of red quill
Body: Flat gold tinsel, ribbed oval gold tinsel
Wing: Grey quill
Beard: Orange hackle

Mallard and Claret

Another old loch fly that has proved its worth on the reservoirs.
Hook: 10, 12 or 14 wet fly
Tail: Golden pheasant tippets
Body: Claret fur (seal)
Rib : Flat gold tinsel
Wing: Dark mallard
Beard: Brown hackle

Invictor

A well-known fly invented in the 1800s. It is said to be a good hatching sedge pattern.
Hook: 10, 12 or 14 wet fly
Tail: Golden pheasant crest
Body: Yellow fur (seal)
Rib : Brown hackle tied palmer
Wing: Brown turkey
Beard: Blue jay

Watson's Fancy

Another respected loch fly that is good for reservoir rainbows.
Hook: 10, 12 or 14 wet fly
Tail: Golden pheasant crest
Body: Claret fur (seal)
Rib : Oval silver tinsel
Wing: Crow quill
Beard: Black hackle

Blae and Black

Possibly an old Irish lough fly, but good for rainbows on reservoirs.
Hook: 10, 12 or 14 wet fly
Tail: Golden pheasant tippets
Body: Black fur (seal)
Wing: Grey quill
Hackle: Black tied palmer

Partridge and Blue

A very similar fly to the popular Partridge and Orange.
Hook: 12, 14 or 16 wet fly
Body: Blue silk (Cambridge blue)
Hackle: Partridge tied as a collar and sloping back

Governor

An American pattern that has proved itself for river trout.
Hook: 12 or 14 wet fly
Tag : Red silk
Body: Wound peacock herl
Wing: Brown mottled turkey
Beard: Brown hackle

Silver Black Gnat

The origin is not known, possibly the USA. A very good river fly.
Hook: 12 or 14 wet fly
Body: Flat silver tinsel
Rib : Oval silver tinsel
Wing: Black crow
Beard: Black hackle

Grannon

A very old underwater sedge pattern.
Hook: 10, 12 or 14 long
Tail: Black hackle fibres
Butt: Green silk built up as an egg sack
Body: Olive/green hare's ear
Wing: Brown turkey
Beard: Brown hackle

Appendix B

Nymph Patterns

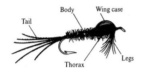

out and the Sub-surface Fly Appendix C 67%

Pheasant Tail

A Sawyer nymph. The basic pattern for all imitative nymphs.
Hook: Regular nymph hook (usually 12 or 14)
Tail: Pheasant tail fibres, usually three
Body: Wound pheasant tail fibres
Rib : Copper wire
Thorax: Wound pheasant tail fibres
Wing Cases: Stretched over pheasant tail fibres

Grey Goose

Another Sawyer nymph. Just as effective as the Pheasant Tail.
Hook: Regular nymph hook
Tail: Grey goose fibres
Body: Wound grey goose fibres
Rib : Copper wire
Thorax: Wound grey goose fibres
Wing Cases: Stretched over grey goose fibres

Cove Pheasant Tail

An Arthur Cove pattern devised for reservoirs.
Hook: 10, 12 or 14 nymph
Body: Wound pheasant tail fibres taken partially round bend of hook
Thorax: Rabbit fur, colour of your choice
Wing Cases: Stretched pheasant tail fibres

Cove Orange

Another Arthur Cove nymph. Popular on the reservoirs.
Hook: 10, 12 or 14 nymph
Tail: 3 pheasant tail fibres
Body: Wound pheasant tail fibres
Thorax: Orange fur
Wing Cases: Stretched pheasant tail fibres
Legs: Orange hackle fibres

Green Collyer Nymph

Devised for fishing the weedy margins of stillwaters.
Hook: Regular nymph hook
Tail: 3 Olive swan fibres
Body: Olive swan fibres
Rib : Copper wire
Thorax: Olive ostrich herl
Wing Cases: Stretched Olive swan fibres

Barry Welham Nymph

An impressionist pattern designed to be fished just below the surface.
Hook: Regular nymph hook
Tail: Short yellow/orange hackle fibres
Body: Brown fur
Rib : Copper wire
Breather Filaments: Short white hackle fibres at the head

Killer Bug

Another Sawyer nymph. Probably represents a shrimp rather than a nymph. Very good for grayling.
Hook: Regular nymph hook
Body: Chadwick 477 wool
Note: Finished nymph has a maggot-style body shape

The Bow Tie

Another Sawyer pattern. Intended to imitate the nymph of the midge. Often called a Buzzer.
Hook: Regular nymph hook
Tail: Pheasant tail fibres, usually 3
Body: Wound pheasant tail fibres
Rib : Copper wire
Thorax: Wound pheasant tail fibres
Breather Filaments: Short bunch of white wool

Stevens Reflector

A pattern of my own. Fully described in the main text.
Hook: Regular nymph hook
Tail: Bunch of long grizzle hackle fibres
Body: Flat gold tinsel
Rib : Oval gold tinsel
Wing Cases: Very short bunch of grizzle hackle fibres
Note: When the body is finished it should be given several coats of clear varnish.

The Stickfly

A very popular stillwater pattern that originated in the UK.
Hook: 10, 12 or 14 long
Tail: Green or yellow floss cut short paintbrush style
Body: Wound peacock herl
Hackle: Ginger, wound as a collar and sloping back

PVC Nymph

An excellent imitation of a pond olive by John Goddard. Can be tied in several ways. This is a popular tying.
Hook: Regular nymph hook
Tail: 3 pheasant tail fibres
Body: Wound pheasant tail fibres overwound with stretched narrow strip of PVC sheeting
Thorax: Wound pheasant tail fibres
Wing Cases: Stretched over pheasant tail fibres

Appendix C

Lure Patterns

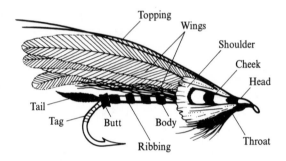

Edson Light Tiger

One of the very best lures for both rainbows and browns. Originated in the USA in 1929 and has a good record.

Hook: 10,12 or 14 long
Tail: Barred wood duck
Tag: Flat gold tinsel
Body: Wound peacock herl
Wing: Yellow hair
Top : Red hackle feather

Little Brown Trout

Brown trout eat their own young! For over 30 years this lure has taken care of the cannibals.

Hook: 14 or 16 long
Tail: Green hair with red floss
Body: Cream fur
Rib : Flat silver tinsel
Wing: 3 bunches of hair: white, orange, green
Throat: Orange

The Missionary

An English lure that originated for Blagdon Lake. Has a proven record.
Hook: 8, 10 or 12 long
Tail: Red hair
Body: White chenille
Rib : Silver tinsel
Wing: Teal feather dressed flat
Throat: Red

Whisky Fly

Another English lure. Originated in the 1970s for reservoir trout. Good in cloudy water.
Hook: 8, 10 or 12 long
Body: Orange floss
Rib : Silver tinsel
Wing: Orange hair
Throat: Orange
Head: Orange

Viva

Origin not known. Very effective for rainbows when fished deep.
Hook: 8, 10, or 12 long
Tail: Green wool
Body: Black chenille
Rib : Silver tinsel
Wing: Black hair

Church Fry

Another 1970s English lure designed for use on reservoirs.
Hook: 8, 10, 12 long
Tail: Green and red hair plus teal feather
Body: White chenille
Rib : Silver tinsel
Wing: White marabou and squirrel tail
Throat: As tail

Muddler Minnow

Everyone knows the Muddler. A Canadian lure that will take fish when others do not produce.
Hook: 8, 10, 12 or 14 long
Tail: Turkey feather
Body: Flat gold tinsel
Wing: Grey squirrel with turkey feather on each side
Shoulders: Spun deer hair clipped to shape

Alexandra

A 1929 English lure of proven record, known the world over.
Hook: 12 or 14 long
Tail: Red Goose
Body: Silver tinsel
Rib : Oval silver tinsel
Wing: Large bunch of peacock herl
Throat: Black hackle

Royal Coachman

The most famous and historic of English patterns. The years have proved its worth.
Hook: 10, 12 or 14 long
Tail: Red goose

Butt: Peacock herl
Body: Scarlet silk
Wing: White swan quill feather
Throat: Brown hackle

Sweeney Todd

A lure designed by the late Dick Walker. Very effective for deep-lying rainbows.
Hook: 10 or 12 long
Body: Black floss, front red floss
Rib : Oval silver tinsel
Wing: Black hair
Throat: Red hackle

Woolly Bugger

Not a specific lure, but a general dressing. A very attractive lure for rainbows. Colour your choice.
Hook: 6, 8, 10 or 12 long
Tail: Marabou, long and bushy
Body: Chenille, colour as tail
Rib : Hackle tied palmer, colour as tail and body

The Thief

Similar to the Muddler but preferred when a smaller lure needed.
Hook: 12 or 14
Tail: Red duck
Body: Silver tinsel
Wing: As Muddler Minnow
Head: Several turns black chenille

Mickey Finn

Probably the best known and popular lure in the USA since it was devised in 1932.
Hook: 10, 12 or 14 long
Body: Flat silver tinsel
Rib : Oval silver tinsel
Wing: Yellow and red hair in three layers – i.e. yellow/red/yellow

Black Ghost

Devised in the USA in 1927. Very widely accepted and very productive.
Hook: 10 or 12 long
Body: Black silk
Rib : Silver tinsel
Wing: White hair
Throat: Yellow hackle

Spruce

A lure of unknown origin from the USA. Several types are tied; this is a very popular one.
Hook: 10 or 12 long
Tail: Bunch of peacock sword fibres
Body: Rear quarter red wool, front three-quarters peacock herl
Wing: Two badger hackles tied back to back to splay out
Throat: Badger hackle wound as a collar

Warden's Worry

Another famous USA lure. Originated in 1930 by a warden in Maine.
Hook: 12 or 14 long
Tag : Flat gold tinsel
Tail: Red duck
Body: Orange/yellow fur
Rib : Oval gold tinsel
Wing: Brown hair
Throat: Yellow

Grey Ghost

A very good UK version of a famous USA lure.
Hook: 8, 10 or 12 long
Tag : Flat silver tinsel
Body: Orange chenille
Rib : Silver tinsel
Wing: White hair
Cheeks: Jungle Cock
Throat: Strands of peacock herl

Christmas Tree

A well-known UK lure designed for reservoir fishing.
Hook: 8, 10 or 12 long
Tail: Green hackle fibres
Body: Black chenille
Rib : Silver tinsel
Wing: Black marabou
Throat: Red hackle

Index